EXCELLENCE IN LEADERSHIP

Excellence in Leadership

Emmanuel Adewusi

CCCG Publishing House

Contents

Dedication		vii
Preface		ix
2	Spiritual Authority	39
3	Humility	73
4	Servant Leadership	96
5	Managing Pressure From Followers	113
6	Avoiding Burnout	132
7	Running With The Vision	149
8	Leading With Love (Part 1)	171
9	Leading With Love (Part 2)	191
10	Emotional Intelligence	215
11	Impartation	243
Epilogue		249
Contact the Author		253
A Sinner's Prayer		255
About the Author		257

Copyright © 2023 Emmanuel Adewusi

All rights reserved. No part of this book may be used or reproduced by any means, graphics, electronic, or mechanical, including photocopying, recording, taping, or by any information storage retrieval system without the author's written permission except in cases of brief quotations embodied in critical articles and reviews.

Scriptures are taken from New King James Version. Copyright 1979, 1980, 1982 by Thomas Nelson, Inc. Used by permission. All right reserved.

Author: Emmanuel Adewusi

ISBN: 978-1-989099-22-3 (hardcover)
ISBN: 978-1-989099-23-0 (ebook)

First Printing 2023

Dedication

This book is dedicated to all those who lead with love and humility, to the servant leaders, those who run with a compelling vision, those who operate under the authority and wisely wield their authority, and to the leaders who take care of themselves as they lead.

Whether you currently occupy a leadership position or aspire to lead with excellence, may this book provide validation, strength, and endurance in your noble service to humanity.

Preface

In a world craving authentic leadership, where the pursuit of success often overshadows the values of integrity and compassion, a voice emerges—one that has witnessed the transformative power of excellence in leadership firsthand. This voice belongs to Emmanuel Adewusi, a seasoned leader, mentor, and advocate for cultivating leaders of character and purpose.

For nearly a decade, Emmanuel has dedicated his life to equipping individuals with the tools, insights, and principles necessary to excel in leadership. Through his basic and advanced leadership classes, he has witnessed the profound impact a leader's character and mindset can have on their ability to inspire, influence, and bring about positive change.

In "Excellence in Leadership," Emmanuel delves into ten fundamental lessons, each essential in unlocking the full potential of leaders driven by a higher purpose. From the battlefield of spiritual warfare to the nuances of emotional intelligence, this book explores a holistic approach to leadership—one that embraces the timeless wisdom found in the teachings of Jesus Christ. The last chapter is one of impartation, for transmitting the grace to lead like Jesus Christ to those who desire it.

"Excellence in Leadership" is not just a compilation of theories and techniques; it is a guide to unlocking the potential within each leader, igniting a fire that propels them towards greatness. Within these chapters, Emmanuel Adewusi weaves timeless biblical principles, practical insights, and real-life examples to provide a comprehensive framework for leadership excellence.

In Lesson 1, Emmanuel exposes the unseen realm of spiritual warfare, guiding leaders through the spiritual battles that inevitably arise on their journey. Lesson 2 unveils the source of true authority and empowers leaders to operate in alignment with Divine guidance and instructions. Lesson 3 uncovers the significance of humility, revealing its transformative power to shape authentic leadership, forge strong connections, and transform the hearts of individuals.

Servant leadership takes center stage in Lesson 4, where Emmanuel demonstrates how leaders who emulate Christ's example can create a lasting impact and empower those they lead. Lesson 5 addresses the pressing challenge of managing pressure from followers, offering practical strategies for maintaining composure and fostering healthy relationships amidst high expectations.

In Lesson 6, Emmanuel acknowledges the reality of burnout and shares essential techniques for self-care, helping leaders find balance and sustainability in their roles. Lesson 7 explores the art of running with the vision, encouraging leaders to persevere, adapt, and stay steadfast in pursuing God-given goals.

Lessons 8 and 9 illuminate the power of leading with love, diving into the depths of empathy, compassion, and kindness as vital components of leadership effectiveness. Lastly, Lesson 10 delves into the realm of emotional intelligence, empowering leaders to navigate their own emotions and establish heartfelt connections with those under their guidance. The final lesson, Lesson 11, ties all the lessons together by exposing leaders to the grace that can make their leadership journey less stressful but highly impactful.

Drawing from his own experiences and the teachings of the Bible, Emmanuel Adewusi presents a roadmap for leadership excellence that transcends personal ambition and focuses on the greater good. This book is not just a collection of theories but a practical guide filled with wisdom, real-life examples, and actionable steps designed to ignite transformation and empower leaders to embrace their calling with passion and purpose.

As you embark on this journey through "Excellence in Leadership," open your heart and mind to the possibilities within you. May these lessons challenge, inspire, and equip you to unleash the leader within—a leader marked by integrity, compassion, and an unwavering commitment to excellence.

Emmanuel Adewusi invites you to embark on a transformational voyage that will empower you to embrace your leadership potential, impact lives, and leave a lasting legacy of excellence. May this book be your trusted companion as you navigate the exhilarating and challenging terrain of leadership, guiding you toward a new level of influence and fulfillment.

1

Spiritual Warfare

Spiritual warfare is an attempt originating from the devil to steal, kill, and/or destroy an individual or group of people's lives or valuables. John 10:10 says, *"the thief does not come except to steal, and to kill, and to destroy."* In that same passage of scripture, Jesus said that He *"came that we may have life and that we may have it more abundantly."* Again, in John 1:4, it was said concerning Jesus that in Him was life, and in His life was the light of men. We have life through Jesus, and we get light from Him.

Think of anything valuable that you have, and I can assure you that it is a target for the devil to steal from you. For example, the devil is after the valuable relationships in your life. People go to bed on good terms with their spouses or children, but they wake up the next day, and the person they made a vow to love is now suddenly seen as dangerous as the devil. The devil's job is to look for valuable things, find ways to steal them, kill a person, and plot ways to destroy them. Since the Garden of Eden, the enemy has focused relentlessly on that mission statement.

Many people can attest that there are times when they go to bed happy but then wake up feeling strange. They explain the feeling away by saying, "I just woke up on the wrong side of the bed." I've been trying to figure out which side of the bed is wrong, and I haven't discovered it yet! It's just a very shallow way of describing the result of the devil's workings during the night. The Bible makes us understand that *"while men slept, his enemy came and sowed tares."* You went to bed happy and woke up just feeling heavy or sad. According to scripture, it is the devil at work.

One of the things that will help us understand the enemy's approach is the realization that the devil does not create anything new. The devil only counterfeits what he sees in the kingdom of God. Some people wake up with anointed songs, and we know that to be the Ministry of the Holy Spirit. The opposite of that is the Ministry of the devil. An example of the Ministry of the devil would be a situation where you come across someone you've never met before, but you dislike that person for no apparent reason.

We see the devil's ammunition on full display in Job 1. This scripture is why some people say that the devil is still one of God's sons, trying to make the devil look good, but that is simply trash. Everything in heaven and on earth still submits to God, directly or indirectly. In that passage of scripture, the devil came to the place where the children of God had gathered. Then God asked the devil where he had been, and he said he was on the earth going to and fro. The question is, what was he doing going to and fro? He was not going around blessing people, but he was on the lookout seeking things to destroy.

He sees two people who are close friends, always happy and praying together, and he thinks to himself, "How can I destroy this relationship?" He wonders, "How come the people I bound in sexual immorality are now sharing testimonies on being set free?" He sees an effective church and people on fire in their service to God and says, "Let's go in there and see how we can mess things up so that they're not as effective as they used to be." He takes note of prosperous people and wonders, "How come this person is making so much, giving so much, doing so many great things, and reaching out to help people? Let's attack their finances." The enemy wants to hear that a church cannot pay for its mortgage or that the people of God are bound in poverty and oppression.

So the devil told God he was going to and fro. Then God asks him, *"Have you considered My servant Job..."* (Job 1:8) Then the enemy answered and said he had seen Job and tried to attack him many times, but there was a hedge of protection around him and everything he owned. God has His eyes on us from the moment we are born. However, just as there is an angel assigned to each person, the devil also assigns demons to watch and observe every person. We saw this in the life of Moses and Jesus Christ. For some people, because of their great destiny, the devil assigns more than one demon to watch them. These demons are what we call familiar spirits. They are the ones who know a person, can speak like them, talk like them, and behave in certain ways like them. These familiar spirits can even think like the person so that, eventually, the person believes that those thoughts are theirs. Those are not your thoughts.

The devil suggested that Job was only serving God because of the blessings that he had received from God. So God allowed the devil to test Job, permitting him to touch anything that Job had, except his life. The life of Job will give you examples and insight into what the devil targets. The devil attacked his health just like he still does today to children of God. The fact that one is growing in age should not mean that they have experience pains, sicknesses, and diseases. Moses grew to be 120 years old, and his eyes and strength were still perfect.

The devil targeted Job's business and all the wealth that he had. He attacked his family. He killed Job's children but did not touch his wife because his wife was working for him by attempting to sow seeds of discouragement into Job. The devil also went further to attack the friendships that Job had as well. Altogether, there were physical, financial, and emotional attacks on Job. Do you know how painful it is to be in a situation where you expect your loved ones to stand by you and comfort you, and they tell you as Job's wife said to Job, to *"Curse God and die!"* or they ask you, "Why are you holding on to your integrity?" In essence, Job's wife was saying, "I don't want you here! You don't have money, and you're not in good health, You're useless to me. Just curse God and die! I don't want you anymore. It would be much better without you being here." In addition, his friends, whom one would expect to know him as a man of integrity, were deeply questioning his integrity. The life of Job is an example of what the enemy does in spiritual warfare.

HOW TO IDENTIFY SPIRITUAL ATTACKS

How do we identify spiritual attacks? There are two extremes that people tend to go to when it comes to identifying spiritual attacks. On one extreme, a person may see a black fly and attribute it to the devil at work. They are quick to say, "Ah! That's the devil!" Some people are on the other extreme, where they trivialize everything. We should not operate on either extreme; there should be a balance. Not every unfortunate incident is the devil. For instance, if someone had something on the stove cooking and they decide to go out, forgetting the food on the stove, and the food gets burnt, there's smoke everywhere, and – God forbid – the house begins to burn down, most likely that was not the devil. It was the person who was irresponsible. So how do we identify that an experience or a situation is a spiritual attack? We can know from two things: **Intensity** and **Frequency**.

Intensity

What do we mean by intensity? Even though every human being can feel sad when something unfortunate happens, there are different levels of sadness. There's a level of sadness called depression, where watching jokes online or listening to music will not lift the individual's spirit. Sadness can come and go on its own, but then depression is one level where sadness just remains. It's a very intense feeling that has the capacity to seemingly paralyze an individual.

How do you gauge intensity? Intensity is relative and is based on the individual's spiritual level. The Bible says that God will not allow us to be tempted beyond our ability to bear. Based on this, we can tell the source of an experience or a situation, whether it is from God or the devil. When something is happening to you that feels unbearable, then you should know that it's a spiritual attack. As stated earlier, intensity is relative because what is intense to one person may not be intense to another person.

Frequency

What do we mean by frequency? As a human living on the earth, you'll occasionally have thoughts that don't glorify God. There is a difference between someone who thinks of stealing once or twice and someone who is bound by a spirit that frequently makes them think of stealing things that don't belong to them. The thoughts of the latter may come like rapid fire and may be very frequent. Those thoughts can come so often that one would begin to recognize it is not normal.

One of the ways you would know that an activity or behaviour is powered by a spirit is that even without human input, it is still happening. It's almost like something else is giving it life. When you see family members, for example, who have been cold toward each other for years, there's likely a spirit involved. 'Something' somewhere is fuelling it. Another example is after hearing a song - you didn't write down the lyrics and may not have paid much attention to it – but it plays continuously in your mind. It came from a spirit, either the Holy Spirit or a demonic spirit. I'll give you another example. Let's say, for instance, you are overworked, and you begin to develop pains in your body, or you hit your leg on a chair, and you start to feel pain.

Everyone develops pains every once in a while, but not all pain is equal. The other day, I did an intense workout and started noticing pains in my leg. Usually, when I experience pain, I lay my hands on the affected area, rebuke it, and then take my mind off it. This one was different because it persisted even after I had prayed and rebuked it. At this point, I asked the Holy Spirit what was going on. He said that the pain in my leg was an attack from the devil. So my next question was,

"What do I do?" He told me what to do. I immediately obeyed, and then the pain disappeared. Now, why was this pain a spiritual attack? It was because of the intensity and the frequency of the pain I was feeling.

Now, let's consider another example of a person whose car tire got punctured by a nail on their way to work on Monday. Nothing too unusual right? These things happen! Anybody who drives their car knows that something like this can happen. But let's say the same thing happened on their way to work on Tuesday; maybe it didn't happen on Wednesday, but it happened again on Thursday. At this point, they should be asking questions. Am I the only one driving? Are there nails just waiting to puncture my tires?! What's going on? Let's look at another scenario where a person woke up in the morning and just didn't feel good. No cause for alarm yet, maybe they ate something bad the night before.

With the understanding that as whole human beings, our body is connected to our soul, which is then connected to our spirit, they decided to pray in the Spirit, but the feeling remained. The feeling intensified throughout the day, and they could not trace why or where it started. This could be a spiritual attack. At every point in time, every child of God is in one of three phases of a spiritual attack:

1. **The Beginning of an Attack**
2. **The Middle of an Attack**
3. **The End of an Attack -You Just Won a Battle!**

If you cannot identify what phase you are in right now, most likely, you are spiritually asleep. We need to understand that any area of your life where things are going well is a potential target for the enemy. On the other hand, in any area of your life where things are not going very well, there is a huge possibility that the enemy is at work there. Why do we say this? Let's go back to the beginning of creation. Life in the

Garden of Eden was a good life. There was food to eat, God's presence was there, and everything worked smoothly until the devil showed up. After this, the pain came, stress came, the curse came, and many other things came that were contrary to the perfection God had created and intended.

Our goal as leaders is to make sure our lives and the lives of those under our authority align with the way God ordained for them to be. No restrictions and no hindrances; that is the ultimate goal from a spiritual warfare perspective. We must build enough strength and gain revelation to go after what the enemy has stolen from us, ensuring complete restoration of everything and guarding against future losses. Remember that we're constantly in a battle, and there are different levels of spiritual warfare.

In Genesis 15, God visited Abraham and told him that a time was coming when his descendants would be in captivity for 400 years. Many years later, the children of Israel went into captivity in Egypt. The 400-year period was God's plan. They were in captivity for 430 years, and so the extra 30 years were the result of a spiritual attack. That was not God's plan. For example, let's say God's plan was for someone to get a job two years after graduation, but then two years passed, and still no job. So why was he still without a job after the two-year timeframe? There's no other explanation for this but the devil. It is also possible that they allowed the devil to play around in their domain through laziness or indolence. It could also be that they were not in support, but the devil overpowered them.

Two dominant forces are at work on the earth, and no middle ground exists. You are either consciously or unconsciously on God's side or the devil's side. Many people work for God without knowing it; on the other hand, many report to the devil without knowing. You are either in God's or the devil's will. When the devil's will prevails in a place or over a person, we say that place or person is under the rule of darkness. When the will of God prevails over a church, family, or community, we say that it is being ruled by the kingdom of light (or heaven), where everything flows the way God has intended it to. This way of life is our ultimate goal, by the grace of God. It is crucial to remember that a spiritual attack aims to draw one away from God instead of closer to Him.

Let's look at different aspects of a human being and how these aspects get attacked by the enemy.

THE PHYSICAL ASPECT

When the enemy launches a spiritual attack against a person's physical body, we know it results in physical sickness, which can manifest in different ways. It can manifest as headaches and pains, and it can also manifest as a lack of something in your physical body that you are supposed to have, like sight or energy. An example of someone under a spiritual attack on their physical body may be a lack of physical energy, so much so that they may have had food to eat but still have no energy.

One of the things that Cornerstone Christian Church of God (CCCG) leadership classes will help us to do is not just to be aware of the enemy's operations but also to get us angry enough to take action when we notice that things we're supposed to have, have been taken from us. Many people are used to approaching spiritual warfare with a defensive posture, but these classes will teach us how to go on the offensive. We have accepted some things as the norm, but we have to get to the point of saying that we don't want them anymore. For example, How could I have slept for eight hours and had breakfast, but at 9 am, I'm feeling very tired? No, no, no. This is unacceptable.

How do we know the benchmark that should govern the functioning of our physical body? We can get those answers from the Bible. Many years ago, I used to have issues with my eyesight. I was on my way to visit a friend in Nigeria when I encountered a group of spiritualists; some call them masquerades. They go around scaring and intimidating people. Usually, when people see them, they run away from them and sometimes give them money. On that fateful day, I was walking to the bus stop, and these masquerades came toward me. I told them to get out of my way, and the masquerade spat something into my eyes that seemed like a palm kernel.

Afterward, my eyes started to bother me. As time went by, it got worse. Over time, I forgot about the incident entirely until many years later, when God reminded me. I love to read, but my eyesight had gotten so bad that after reading for 30 minutes, I had to forcibly rest my eyes for at least an hour before I could go back to reading. I consulted with opticians and ophthalmologists, and they all said the same thing, that I was reacting to particles in the air. No one could supply a solution; it all seemed like they were taking guesses. A wicked family member who saw the pain that I was in even suggested that I put pepper in my eyes, as he had watched it on some show. Eventually, I moved to Poland and decided to see some doctors about the issue. They said the same thing that the doctors in Nigeria had said; that I was reacting to particles in the air.

A couple of years after I moved to Canada, the doctors said the same thing. The doctors prescribed eyeglasses that didn't help at all. I had spent so much time seeking help from doctors over the issue that I accepted it at some point, until one day when I read Deuteronomy 34:7, *"And Moses became 120 years old, and his eyes did not dim, neither was his natural force abated."* I asked myself, "How can a man be 120 years old and have no eye pains?" I was 20-something then and decided that this could not be. But that day, when I read that scripture, I remember going on my knees and asking God to perfect my eyes. Before then, once I woke up in the morning, the first thing I would feel was the pain in my eyes, and that's when I knew it was time to get up for the day. A day after that prayer, I woke up, and I knew something was different;

after a few seconds, I realized there weren't any pains in my eyes, and I had been healed.

The way to know God's benchmark for us is by connecting with the Word of God, and not the people around us. Several stories in the Bible will give every one of us a picture of what good health is. You can choose to pick your standard from the Bible. You can also use other people's bad experiences around you as your examples by saying things like, "Oh, I know this Pastor who died at this young age, so it's not bad to die at that age" or "I know this person who was a very strong believer, but she always had bad migraines, so it's not a big deal to have migraines."

The devil can target a person's body, so we need to always be spiritually aware. If you don't learn to fight against the little things that the devil brings your way, you will soon notice that those things will grow to become something that is way more than you can handle. I hear people say, "Oh, it's just a little pain in this area, but it's fine, it's fine," but then the little pain – if it is from the devil – could eventually become something that will require deliverance. When you notice discomfort in your body, even if it is a little headache, rebuke it in the name of Jesus because you have control over your body, and then you move on.

THE SOUL ASPECT

The human soul comprises **Emotions**, **Will**, and **Mind**.

Emotions

The devil can attack people's emotional lives. What benchmark should govern our emotional well-being? God always wants the fruit of the Spirit to be at work in our lives, "*love, joy, peace, longsuffering, kindness, goodness, faithfulness, gentleness, self-control.*" (Galatians 5:22-23) The idea is that every one of the items listed should always be at work in a person's life.

How would you know that a person's emotions are being attacked? You know there's an attack when the person finds it hard to love people. How do you know that you are genuinely loving people? You can forgive, you can give, and you can tolerate people. However, when your emotions are under attack, you just feel like everyone is irritating, and the feelings will be very intense and frequent.

Many things can affect our ability to love at different points in time as human beings. If you find that even after removing all those hindrances, you're still constantly irritated by others, and continually pointing out their mistakes, then your emotions are likely under attack. The absence of the ability to love means there's an attack on the person's emotional life. I don't have to like someone before I can love someone. The grace to love has been given to us by God, as we know from Romans 5:5, *"The love of God has been poured abroad in our hearts by the Holy Spirit."* Therefore, if a person finds that they need an excuse or a valid reason to love a person, then their emotional life is under attack.

You might wonder, how one would balance the difference between constantly having feelings of irritation toward people and loving people, while still not liking what they do. You can love a person, but not feel obliged to be friends with them, which is okay. A lot of what we humans define as love is actually likeness. Should we blame Hollywood, Bollywood, Nollywood, and all the woods for this? I don't know! But did Jesus like the Pharisees? No. He loved them, but He didn't 'like' them.

We're not talking about the Jesus people make up in their minds. We're talking about the 'real' Jesus that we read about in scripture. The Bible records that Jesus was irritated by His disciples sometimes because they would ask questions He already expected them to know. Jesus would say, *"I've been with you for so long, and you still do not understand..."* (John 14:9-11). Jesus did not like the Pharisees and the Sadducees, He loved them. It was evident that He loved them in the way that He spoke to them. *"For God so loved the world, that He gave His only begotten Son..."* (John 3:16). That is why when Nicodemus, who used to be one of them, decided to step out and come to Jesus, He received him. This is a good test to know if you love someone; If you were the only one who could donate blood to them because they would die, would you do it?

Love has nothing to do with feelings. Love can impact your feelings, but feelings are not always a good test of love. In most of our relationships, what we call love is really just lust, because the moment the physical shape, the money, or the things that endeared us to that person disappears, the 'love' disappears. If love disappears, then maybe it was never love in the first place. Any attempt by the devil to impact our ability to love people is an attack on our emotional lives.

Let's assume that a person was attacked spiritually and the person was unable to fight back and remained subdued; if that person went ahead to have children, then they would raise their offspring in a subdued state. You cannot give what you don't have. A bad tree will bear bad fruit, and a good tree will bear good fruit. For example, some people – through no doing of their own – grow up to become angry people, because the anger trait was passed from a previous generation and baked into their upbringing. God didn't create angry people, but because they were raised by an angry parent, and they saw a lot of anger growing up, they now respond to every inconvenience with anger.

Compare that to somebody else who was raised in a completely different environment. That is why Jesus said, *"from the beginning it was not so."* (Matthew 19:8) Therefore, somewhere along the line, the enemy came and planted something evil that nobody was powerful enough to shut down, so it just continued. Jesus came to do a great reset, and so once we tap into Christ, we are able to reset the things that the devil has bastardized and polluted. So spiritual warfare is not just when a person had a bad dream or a bad encounter. The depth of spiritual warfare is that even in a state of peace, you ask yourself, "What has contributed to what I am today that is not of God?" We must go deep into the root.

Let's take diabetes as an example. Most people who have it would know that when you go to the doctor's office, they will ask you if there is anybody from your family who has it. Why? Because even doctors themselves are aware that attacks can be transmitted from one generation to another. But my question to you is: Did Adam or Eve have diabetes? No, but somewhere along the line, something happened that introduced diabetes into a lineage and just began to get passed down from generation to generation and until one person decides that this thing must stop here, it will just keep getting passed down. Cataracts and all kinds of things will get passed down until one person stands their ground and fights back and now their offspring will be shielded from those things.

Let me point something out; please pay close attention here. Remember that I mentioned earlier that everyone is at the beginning, middle, or end of an attack (if you succeeded in dealing with it). For many people, the attacks started before birth and have continued because it hasn't been shut down yet. The enemy's goal is for an attack to become the norm for the individual under attack and even for their generations to come. The enemy is interested in having attacks baked into a culture so deeply that it is being transmitted automatically from one generation to the next. I'll give you an example, 'men don't cry.' This is a normative statement that serves as an example of an emotional attack that originated from a time in the past and has now become so deeply rooted in society and across many generations. Even the Bible records that "*Jesus wept.*" (John 11:35) The idea that 'men don't cry' is a poison that has been passed through generations, and is still being received to this day by some people, while some others have been delivered from it and are living free.

Consider this question, "Are anger, impatience, sexual immorality, and so on, generational curses?" The answer is simple. If they persist and continue outside a person's control, then we can say that they are generational curses. A generational curse is a spiritual attack that starts with somebody and is passed down to every member or person in that lineage who receives it. Every time something ceases to go the way God has ordained, instead of being a blessing, it becomes a curse. Instead of being a positive addition, it adds negative things and takes away good things.

Will

Some people find it very difficult to make decisions. Things as little as figuring out what to wear can, at that moment, cripple them, causing the individual to be stressed over being unable to make the decision. We are decision-making beings. An average human being makes hundreds of decisions daily. When a person reaches a point where suddenly decision-making gets difficult and near impossible, the enemy may be behind it.

Indecisiveness is an attack of the enemy over your will. Have you encountered people with all the information they need to make a decision but cannot find themselves pulling the trigger? Do you remember that Jesus specifically said, *"But let your 'Yes' be 'Yes,' and your 'No,' 'No.' For whatever is more than these is from the evil one."* (Matthew 5:37) This scripture explains that whatever hinders you from being decisive, saying yes when you mean yes or saying no when you mean no, is orchestrated by the evil one. I declare that every attack over your will is neutralized in Jesus' mighty name.

Mind

The enemy can sometimes come after an individual's mind. Our minds are designed to receive, process, disseminate, and store information. Anything that seeks to cripple this normal functioning of the mind is not from God and could be the work of the enemy. Understand that there are times when individuals break biblical principles for the correct use of their minds. In most cases, however, a person's mind can be bombarded with thoughts contrary to their nature. Suddenly rebellious thoughts can flood an individual's mind, and if they are not careful, they may take ownership of those thoughts, leading them to rebellious actions and eventually destruction.

For some people, the attack is on their ability to process information. The information they received was good and pure, but they somehow came to an inappropriate and unusual conclusion that does not line up with the given input. You may tell and show them that you love them, but one way or the other, they will come up with a strange interpretation of your show of love that will eventually cause them to avoid you instead of drawing closer to you. In this case, the enemy has set up hindrances in their ability to understand or comprehend the truth. This strange behaviour often manifests when the mind is exposed to the truth. They find it difficult, if not impossible to understand the truth.

According to 2 Corinthians 4:4, the god of this world, satan, has intentionally blinded their ability to comprehend the truth. When they hear the testimonies of God's acts, their immediate response is that it is untrue. They, however, find it easy to believe fictional movies and go on about how those depictions in movies perfectly align with reality and should be trusted. In the peculiar case of others, they can hear the truth and even believe it. The mental attack they face is the inability to disseminate this truth accurately.

Much of our interactions as humans are through verbal and non-verbal communication. A person may think that they have a good grasp on a subject matter but may find it crippling to share what they know with others, either in spoken or written form. Their minds suddenly become flooded with irrational ideas that limit them from sharing the truth they know. One of the lies they may have received from the enemy is that they are shy or timid. These ideas are lies from the pit of hell. If you can talk with your friends, family, etc., you can talk to anyone else. I declare your liberty and lose your tongue right now in Jesus' name. Whatever aspect of your mind you find has been attacked by the enemy, understand that you can be set free now at this very moment.

THE SPIRITUAL ASPECT

An attack on one's spiritual life is the height of all spiritual attacks. If a snake bites a person, the goal of the venom is to try to get to the heart. In the same way, the goal of any spiritual attack is to get a person to the point where they deny Christ. That's why Job's wife said to him, *"Curse God and die..."* (Job 2:9). Why did she have to say 'curse God'? She could have just told him to kill himself, but cursing God is denying God.

Oppression vs Possession

When it has to do with spiritual attacks, it begins with oppression. Oppression simply means that a force is trying to control a person. From the very beginning of time, the devil's goal has always been to control humans. Romans 8:14 says, *" As many as are led by the spirit of God, they are the children of God."* God wants to be in charge of our affairs. The devil's goal, too, is to control and to be the one who determines what a person thinks, what they do, and what they don't do, and he even wants to talk through that person. Thus oppression comes as an external force, putting pressure to gain control over an individual. Demonic suggestions and anything contrary to the will of God are usually communicated to a person with intense pressure from the outside.

If a person fails to resist oppression, it can evolve to become a possession. Possession is when demons can talk through their victim without the victim's permission. When we fail to fight back in the face of oppression or lose the battle to oppression, it will eventually degenerate into possession. At this point, that person fully becomes an agent of the devil.

Think of demons as worms. Worms can be around a person's environment, plaguing them (oppression), but once you find the worms inside that person, it's a sign that the person has died (possession).

That's why it is very important that we build up spiritual strength. People conform to demonic pressure not because they want to conform, but because the grace and the strength to fight back are lacking. So they become agents of the devil, where the devil can talk through them to oppress people, causing them to say things they ought not to have said.

After such episodes, they begin to ask themselves, "Why am I talking like this?" but they cannot control themselves or prevent themselves from acting or speaking in such a manner. That is demonic possession. Another example of demonic possession is when a person blacks out and is unaware of their actions for a moment. So when a person, because of anger, does not know they were acting in a certain way for 5 or 10 minutes, who was controlling them? That's a demon or demons.

The more a person falls to oppression, the quicker they reach a threshold where they could lose control of themselves. You will hear them say things like, "What's the point? I've already tried; I might as well just give up." Human agency means that as human beings, we are capable of making decisions. So the moment that power is no longer there, you begin to do what you don't want to do, like being an enslaved person controlled by their master. This is a picture of someone who is possessed already. So, oppression and possession are two states of spiritual attack. One is more like the beginning stage, and the other is the goal of the enemy. We see why the devil told Jesus to jump when he was tempting Jesus. He wanted to get to the point where he could tell Christ what to do.

You might wonder if a born-again Christian can be possessed and still be considered a Christian. When John the Baptist died, Jesus took time off to spend with God. There are certain points in a person's journey where they will be vulnerable to attacks they would typically not have been vulnerable to. When you hear of people who had been fervently and passionately preaching against homosexuality, and then down the line, they got caught in some dirty place or hotel with the same sex, then you would know that the grace of God that is keeping all of us.

Though the madman of Gadara in Matthew 5 was possessed, he still came and bowed down to Jesus. If the devil gets a hold of a person's agency, which is the center of their will, they can no longer be referred to as a Christian. To become born-again, one must believe that Jesus is Lord in their heart and declare with their mouth. If demons can make that same person declare with their mouth that they are no longer submitted to Christ, then they are no longer saved. The truth is, once demons possess a person, denouncing Christ is something that can easily happen.

It is not a sign of weakness if a person is oppressed. The enemy can attack and put pressure on anybody. That is why the Bible says, *"If you faint in the day of adversity, Your strength is small."* (Proverbs 24:10) If a person yields to the oppressive nature of an attack, it is because the strength they had or the strength they had access to was small (or weak, as the Bible puts it). It is, therefore, important for children of God to have devotions daily, to walk in righteousness every day, and to repent and get back on track when they miss the mark. Attacks can come at any point in time.

Spiritual Discernment

We do not glorify the devil, but it is also unwise to completely underestimate the devil. There has to be a good understanding of an opponent to continually remain the dominant force. That is why every military or government has intelligence services to evaluate the strengths and weaknesses of their opponents and build capabilities to stay on top.

As Christians, we must intentionally build our relationship with God and meditate on scripture as He builds our strength to remain ahead of the enemy's schemes. The devil has been around for a long time and has many tools in his arsenal to attack God's children.

Imagine a man suddenly deciding that he doesn't love his wife anymore and there is a colleague at his place of work that is just the best in his opinion because he's had one or two conversations with her, and she seems to understand him. This is an attempt by the devil to destroy his marriage, and this is an example of oppression. When the devil brings such suggestions, we must fight back by saying, "No, I rebuke you in Jesus' name." It might continue for weeks or months, or what may seem like a long time, but eventually, it will disappear.

On the other hand, a weak person may begin to give it some thought and start to accept the idea, looking for ways to feed this new relationship with their colleague. The next thing you may hear is that they poisoned their spouse, falling straight into the trap of the enemy. We build strength for the day of battle because there will always be a day of battle for everybody.

Now, along the same line, every domain has principalities and powers that have been assigned to handle those domains. Depending on where we are, the kinds of forces we have access to and the forces we have to deal with will vary.

Many years ago, while working for a consulting company, I travelled to Vancouver for work. A barrage of sexual thoughts flooded my mind immediately after I landed at the airport. When you have control over the thoughts flowing through your mind, you will be aware when something different and unusual comes in. I immediately started to rebuke it, while at the same time, I was wondering what was going on.

By the time I got to the hotel I was supposed to stay, it had become more intense. Moments later, I decided to go out and get some food. This was downtown and at night. Suddenly, some people driving by in a car stuck their necks out of the car and shouted, "Sex! Sex! Do you want to have sex?" I thought, "What kind of place is this??" Then I directed my questions to my Helper, the Holy Spirit, and He said, *"Don't you know where you are? One of the spiritual forces at work in this place is the spirit of sexual immorality."*

It may differ for different locations, so it is important to always be spiritually alert. For Vancouver, the forces at work are sexual immorality and drug addiction. If your eyes are open, the signs will be everywhere once you step into that domain, and when I say 'eyes open,' I don't mean physical eyes but your spiritual eyes.

One day in Edmonton, I was driving to work downtown, and the Holy Spirit asked me, *"Do you know the spiritual forces at work here?"* I said that I didn't know, so He told me, *"The spirit of rationalization and the love of money."* I understood the love of money but didn't understand the rationalization part. He then further explained that the spirit of rationalization makes people say, "I won't believe anything until I see evidence," which is simply the opposite of faith.

If you think about it, that way of thinking makes no sense! When you work, your employer tells you they will pay your salary to a bank every two weeks, and you believe them without asking for evidence that they will not fail to do so. When it comes to God, even after people hear testimonies, they find it very hard to believe.

A geographical domain consists of people, families, and individuals. There are certain forces at work over some families. When a person moves into a particular domain, they can begin to battle with something they never struggled with before. So immediately when I landed in Vancouver, I had to take steps to ensure that I was not compromised during my time there. It is one of the reasons why distractions are very dangerous.

We said earlier that one of the ways to know spiritual attacks other than asking the Holy Spirit is by looking at the frequency and intensity of an occurrence. This draws on our ability to study patterns. For example, think of some things that flow through your family lineage that you know are not of God.

Some people don't know that their great-grandmother gave birth to their grandmother at the age of 18 without being married and that the same thing happened to their grandmother and also to their mother. Suddenly, the same pattern is beginning to repeat itself. It may seem apparent to a person whose eyes are open spiritually, but not everybody can point out such patterns because they are distracted by life.

Some people are not aware that the pattern in their family is poverty. They are a family or a generation of hard-working people, but you can't point out anybody in their lineage who has not had to live from paycheque to paycheque. For other people, there may be an age when people in the family die, just like that. Distractions keep us from being aware of such evil patterns. God said to me a few years ago, *"Join me in declaring war against distractions."*

At the beginning of any new year, some people just go into a state of slumber, and the next time they become aware of themselves, it is already the end of the year. They keep going through the motions, activity after activity. It seems like the whole year was just a blur because they went through it distracted. When there are no distractions, we become increasingly aware of things happening around us; we can take note of patterns and anything out of place and shut them down.

Let's assume a person is used to being honoured wherever they go, but they went to a particular place and were treated dishonourably; they then went somewhere else again, and it happened again. Assuming this happens a couple more times, a person who understands and is sensitive to patterns will pause and ask God, "Okay, God, is there something happening here? Have I missed something somewhere?" Once revelation is received, one can easily take steps so that things begin to work the way they are supposed to.

Still closely linked with discernment is the ability to see the influences on people close to you and its possible impact on you. For example, a spiritual attack on a family member or a close friend can be transferred to you by physical proximity or heart/emotional proximity. The way it happens in the physical realm is the way it happens in the spiritual realm, and I'll give you an example.

In the physical realm, if a person has the flu, without conscious effort, they can pass it on to as many people as possible. That's how it is also spiritually. A person under attack by the spirit of anger, for instance, who does not take steps to shut down the operation of that spirit, can inflame anger in other people they come across. People around them may start to feel that anger, especially if those people are not spiritually sensitive as well. They feel it because someone who carried that spirit came into the environment. Irritation is anger; it's just not as intense as anger yet. It takes discernment to identify irritation before it becomes full-fledged anger!

Dominating the Body

We have to learn quickly as Christians to dominate our bodies. Topics surrounding what to eat or what not to eat are elementary things. Another aspect of our being that we need to dominate is our minds. Anyone who has not learned to dominate these two will be very restricted in their spiritual growth. What do you like to listen to every day? It's up to you. We need to put systems in place that will enforce habits to ensure that we are constantly and continuously in charge of our bodies and minds. A lifetime is not enough for spiritual exploration. The Bible says, *"Therefore if you have not been faithful in the unrighteous mammon, who will commit to your trust the true riches?"* (Luke 16:11-12) Some people have not even begun spiritual exploration; they're still struggling in the physical dimension of life.

There will always be a constant battle in a particular domain for what kingdom will dominate. It depends on which side is more powerful. Spiritual exercises like fasting and meditating on scripture give us the energy required to dominate. Not engaging in such practices, leaves us drained with no energy to fight. The devil has been fasting from the beginning, and he is still fasting; it is all about how much strength one can build.

In Mark 9, when the disciples tried to cast out the deaf-and-dumb spirit from the boy and they couldn't, they went to Jesus afterward, and He told them that, *"this kind [of demon] does not go out except by prayer and fasting."* (Matthew 17:19-21) It means that unless someone has developed a lifestyle of fasting, they cannot have that kind of power to cast out a demon like that. Further, it means that someone who will operate with such power has dominated their body or urges of the flesh.

There are levels and phases to gaining spiritual power. It is why there is always fasting involved on the path to empowerment because God is saying to dominate your body. You know you're hungry. Usually, you'd go to get something to eat, but you don't because you are on the path to dominating your body. The Bible says that *"He who descended is also the One who ascended..."* (Ephesians 4:10), and so to be able to ascend into higher levels of spiritual authority, we must die to the flesh. So many people rely on their physical energy to get things done, so it is important to eliminate dependence on the flesh.

There is also emotional fasting. When God takes a person through the wilderness season, that is emotional fasting. We might not call for an emotional fast as a church, but God takes every individual who must ascend spiritually through it. He may separate friends from them and make them feel isolated. This is called an emotional fast. Unfortunately, many people do not allow God to take them through this, and instead, they keep clinging to people who God is trying to separate them from, so they never dominate in this area. God told Abraham to leave his father's house; that was an emotional fast.

Revelation

Earlier, we defined a spiritual attack as anything originating from the devil to steal, kill, and destroy. The only way we can effectively have victory over a spiritual attack is by 'light'. And when I say light, I mean 'revelation'. It is not necessarily fasting and prayer, but light. I have seen people spend the whole night trying to cast out a demon, but all they are doing is simply intense physical exercise because, by morning, the demon is still there. I have seen people simply speak the Word, and demons leave. I decided that I wanted to be in the latter category.

There's a difference between deliverance and freedom. Deliverance means, "I've cast out a demon from a person." That means it's no longer bothering them. Freedom, however, is when the demon cannot come back. Freedom can only be obtained when 'light' comes into the individual. And by light, I mean they're now operating by a different set of principles that will make that spirit unable to return. That's when they can be truly free.

Jesus made us understand that when a spirit is cast out of a person, it will go through dry places, looking for a place to rest. If it finds none, it will say to itself, *"I will return to my house from which I came."* (Matthew 12:44) If he goes back and sees his original place is swept clean but empty, then he will find seven more powerful spirits, and they will come back and dwell in that person, then the latter end of that person will be way more destructive than the beginning. It is why I don't rush to cast out spirits from people. If I cannot sit down with them and show them the 'light', then it is better to leave them the way they are.

I'm a mathematician. If there is just one right now, and I quickly cast out that one, and don't have time to teach them how to live their lives so they can remain free, then I am endangering them. They will live free, but only for a short period of time. I can assure you that Jesus is not a liar, and seven more powerful demons will come back with the first, and it will be way more difficult to get that person free. So based on that, I'm not in a haste to cast out the demon because I love that person.

People love to attend deliverance conferences but find it difficult to sit down and listen to Bible studies to learn and grow. People would rather pray for 6 hours than read their Bible for 6 hours when reading to get 'light' is way more beneficial than praying without 'light'. I've seen people fast for 40 days or 21 days, but ended up worse than they started because there was no 'light'; the light from the Word was missing. They will pray, but if they were asked to quote some basic life principles, they couldn't. They know how to rebuke the devil from their finances, but if you ask them about giving and other Biblical principles on prosperity, they are unaware of those things, even though these are elementary principles in the Bible. Even non-believers are more aware of those principles in some cases.

When you realize that the state of affairs around you is not the way God ordained it, you must take action, starting with yourself. Jesus said in Luke 4:23 that we will tell a parable, *"Physician, heal yourself."* So deliverance begins from within ourselves. Moses could go back to set

Israel free because he was free. Deliverance has to happen before the people being delivered can now go and get light for themselves. Deliverance can only be administered by an external force that is greater than what is holding the person bound. That force has to be free themselves because the blind cannot lead the blind. When the person is delivered, they have a period of time to go and get the revelation they need to stay free.

I'll give you an example. Let's say we have a person bound by the spirit of anger, and someone has rebuked that spirit from them and delivered them; the next step will be to sit them down and show them principles on how to deal with offence because people will still offend them. Now they learn the principles. Previously, when they were angry, they would sit on it and let it fester until an outburst occurs. Now, they have principles they can apply to ensure they remain free.

One of such principles is found in the Bible and it says, *"Moreover if your brother sins against you, go and tell him his fault between you and him alone. If he hears you, you have gained your brother. But if he will not hear, take with you one or two more, that 'by the mouth of two or three witnesses every word may be established.' And if he refuses to hear them, tell it to the church. But if he refuses even to hear the church, let him be to you like a heathen and a tax collector."* (Matthew 18:15-17) So those are higher principles that we follow as believers. For those that have revelation, when anger tries to come, it won't stay anymore because they know the higher principles to follow. If they don't follow those principles, the spirit of anger will still come back because the truth is you can't stop people from offending you; that's life.

Once the person is free, then the only people they have the power to set free are the people under their authority. So, for instance, if you are the youngest in the family, then you don't have the spiritual authority over the rest of your family to say, "Okay, demon, I cast you out of my whole family." No. The father might want that demon in themselves, and you don't have the power to take away his decision to want the demon to remain there. If the father is free, however, he can decide that the demon can no longer operate in their home. A mother can also make that kind of decision.

If you look at the story of Lazarus, he couldn't make decisions for himself because he had died, and the Bible didn't say anything about his parents. Hence, the next person who had authority was Martha, and we can decipher that Martha was the older sibling between him and Mary when we read through their story. Therefore, Martha had the authority to ask Jesus to bring Lazarus back to life. If a husband, for example, is in a coma, the wife or his parents have the authority to say, "No, we want him back." Now, this principle of spiritual authority is not always based on age.

Esau, for example, handed over his birthright to Jacob, so spiritually, Jacob was now head over Esau. Therefore, Jacob could make decisions on behalf of Esau spiritually, and it would have been honoured spiritually. So it's not just about age. As a Pastor, I have spiritual authority over the members, regardless of their age. When someone comes to Cornerstone and says that they want to be a member and that Cornerstone is where they belong, then they come under God's authority in me. When I pray for the church members, even the devil knows that individual is a part of the prayer.

A person can also decide that they are taking themselves out from under my authority. They might still be serving, but in their heart, they are no longer a part of the church. Then my prayers no longer cover them. Many of the decisions to remain under authority or take ourselves from under authority happen in our minds. The prodigal son decided to come back under the authority of his father. That decision caused the father to wait for him at the entrance. He knew in his spirit that this boy was coming back because of the decision he had already made. *"For with the heart one believes unto righteousness, and with the mouth confession is made unto salvation."* (Romans 10:10) Many of us are making decisions in our minds which are being recorded; hopefully, they are good decisions.

A younger person or one without authority over their household can bring restoration to a whole family through teaching and sharing the 'light' of God's Word, even though they do not have the authority to rebuke the operations of demonic spirits in that home. The younger one can begin to teach the parents subtly and wisely by introducing them to 'light'. Once the elders receive it and start walking in it, the deliverance can come from the top. This is the most important aspect of spiritual warfare, acquiring principles to ensure that 'light' remains in place. Truly, walking in Divine principles is the apex of spiritual warfare.

In Matthew 4, we saw the story of Jesus facing the devil. Not everyone will be privileged to face the devil in one-on-one combat. We attribute everything to the devil, but the devil can only be in one place at a time. Only God is omnipresent. The devil has a system of agents. So when the devil was tempting Jesus, that was the only place where the devil was at that time. The devil only appears and deals with places and people directly related to the return of Christ, but there are principalities, powers, and rulers of darkness everywhere.

When the devil met with Jesus, Jesus was not screaming and shouting. All He said was, *"It is written..."* (Matthew 4:4). That is spiritual warfare. And quoting scripture is not the same as having a revelation, which is 'light'. I know a guy who was running away from the devil, but he kept quoting, *"For God has not given us a spirit of fear, but of power and of love and of a sound mind."* (2 Timothy 1:7) Thus it's not about regurgitating scriptures; it's actually about saying what you 'believe' in your heart.

I was going to minister somewhere on a Sunday morning. The night before, I was preparing, and dancing in my room, when suddenly I bent down, and my back became stiff. I was unable to straighten my back to get back up again, and the pain was excruciating. At that moment, all kinds of thoughts went through my mind. There, I remembered a few months prior, I was listening to my spiritual father, who quoted Colossians 2:15, *"Having disarmed principalities and powers, He made a public spectacle of them, triumphing over them in it."* I never sat down to memorize it, but at that moment, that scripture was fired into my spirit.

Being in that bent position seemed like forever, but it was just a few seconds. That scripture just came to mind, and from my spirit (because out of the abundance of the heart, the mouth speaks), I just began to say, "Having disarmed principalities and powers, He made a public spectacle of them, triumphing over them by the cross. Satan get your hands off my back, in the name of Jesus!" The pain immediately lifted, and I was able to stand upright. Real spiritual warfare is fighting with truth, with light, and with revelation.

I'm not afraid of anyone or anything; I have been delivered from fear, but there was a time when there was so much pressure to be afraid, and it was intense. The moment I understood what was happening, I declared, *"For God has not given [me] a spirit of fear, but of power and of love and of a sound mind."* (2 Timothy 1:7) You spirit of fear, I rebuke you in the name of Jesus.

When we say that dealing with spiritual warfare involves 'light', I mean 'light' in two primary ways:

1. **The Revealed Word of God**
2. **The Written Word of God**

THE REVEALED WORD OF GOD

Revelation of Who or What You're Dealing With

Every time Jesus fought warfare, He mentioned the name of what He was dealing with. *"Get thee behind me, Satan,"* or *"you deaf-and-dumb spirit."* There was only one time when He didn't mention the name, and that's when He asked, *"...what is your name?"* (Mark 5:9) This was in Mark 5 with the madman of Gadara, and the demon said, *"...my name is Legion, for we are many."* (Mark 5:9) Then He cast out the spirit!

The problem that most people have when they are rebuking and nothing is happening is that they're not sure what they are dealing with. One moment, you think it's the spirit of anger. Another moment, you think it is because you've not eaten; another moment, you think it was someone else's fault. The Bible says that the double-minded will receive nothing from God, but when revelation comes, you'll know the exact spirit you are dealing with and you'll be certain that you are targeting the root of the issue. Because you have identified what it is, the spirit will know you are operating at a different level. God responds according to our level of faith, but sometimes we enjoy the mercy of God. Sometimes, someone else's prayer may be doing the work.

If we're unsure of what spirit we are dealing with, is it okay to ask the demon for its identity, or was that just something only Jesus could do? I would not recommend conversing with demons. From a scriptural perspective, we can only consider something to be a doctrine when there is a record of its occurrence two or more times. Jesus never did that again; it only happened once, according to scripture. We cannot take what God did to Job as a doctrine because it only happened to Job and no one else in scripture. So if a voice says to you because of a season you are going through, "Maybe you are Job", you should say,

"I rebuke you in Jesus' name." You can accept that as a doctrine if it happened two or more times.

A doctrine is a way of life in the kingdom of God. I'll tell you a true life story. A group of people were trying to cast out a demon from a person. They asked the demon to tell them how many other demons were present in that individual. The spirit mentioned a number, let's say ten. So the group began to rebuke the demons. To gauge their progress, after an hour, they asked the demon how many they were, and it said, "We are nine." They continued for a while and then asked the demon again; the demon then said they were 20. Suddenly, one of them received spiritual illumination, told everyone to stop, and declared that they were dealing with a lying spirit. In light of that revelation, the individual declared with boldness, "You lying spirit, I rebuke you in the name of Jesus," and the spirit left immediately.

THE WRITTEN WORD OF GOD

There is a principle to follow to ensure a demon doesn't come back. Let's assume a person's family was previously bound by the spirit of poverty, where they worked very hard, but nobody was rising past a certain level. Now, that spirit has been rebuked, and God gives that person revelation of the principles for prosperity. The person begins to practice the principles of prosperity, and resources begin to come. They are no longer under attack, but the Bible says, *"let him who thinks he stands should take heed lest he fall."* (1 Corinthians 10:12) So it is now about diligently following and practicing those principles to ensure that the spirit of poverty stays away.

For example, let's consider the principle of walking in love. I've been to some places where the Pastor knew that two people in the congregation were not talking to each other but didn't do anything about it until pockets of offence started to spread among the members, and people began to form cliques. Therefore, they've made that place an infestation of demonic spirits because of inaction to deal with the root cause. Does everybody have to like everybody? No, but the offence must never be allowed to remain in a place because it goes against the principles of walking in love.

We should always be in pursuit of 'light' - principles. If you want to withstand spiritual warfare in any area, you must have a revelation from God on how to thrive in that area. Otherwise, it is just a matter of time before the devil takes hold of that area. You must understand that there is a period between when a person has been delivered and when they must learn principles to prevent themselves from being repossessed.

Time is another concept on its own in terms of spiritual exploration. Time is dependent on the individual, God's purpose, where the devil is, and the geographical area. It's a complex concept on its own. The Bible says, *"Now is the accepted time."* (2 Corinthians 6:2) Today is the day of salvation. When you hear, don't harden your heart. What we should focus on is, at that moment, once the revelation comes, move with it as quickly as possible. Trying to decipher certain things about time can be like playing in muddy water.

Sometimes people come to me and ask if the person they're already married to is God's perfect will for them. I rarely answer those questions because if they are already married, how would that information benefit them? Yet even when I know the acceptable will of God can still give them a good life, I would not share that information. Due to a lack of understanding, any unbearable situation will cause them to think, "Yeah, this was not the perfect will. That's why this is happening," and they would be unable to fight back the way they ought to fight back. Therefore, some things you let be, and the moment your revelation comes, your job is to act on it, and all will be well.

I pray that God will open your eyes to see the things that you must take back that have been stolen from you through no fault of your own. Even if it was your fault, we must begin to take steps to get those things back. In many cases, we may have to consult with someone higher than us, read books, or connect with anointed messages because finding 'light' is a very costly endeavour. If it were easy, everybody would have access to it, but once you find it, you found it!

There was a testimony, for example, about a person who was told to identify people who loved them. It sounds very simple, but I can tell you that it is not that simple when people don't understand it. How can a person in a world with billions of human beings say that they are lonely? It makes no sense, but that is many people's reality. I can assure you that there are people who love that person dearly, but to them, nobody loves them, and they are sure that this is true. So that's why we pursue 'light'.

Someone was asking me before the Ministry started why deliverance was not part of our 12 cornerstones. My answer was that, when you see 'the Word of God' among the twelve cornerstones, understand that it includes deliverance. Every time you interact with God's Word, you're being delivered and kept free. Revelation and practice of the Word are the best ways, in my own opinion, to remain free. Spiritual warfare is real.

I heard of someone's experience after a prayer session. She was heading home, and these voices started oppressing her and told her to drive her car into an oncoming train. She started crying, and it got to a point where she was already going in the direction of the train. Spiritual warfare can mean life or death. Life does not leave a person just like that; it is taken. Either God requests it, or the devil takes it because the person could not resist him. Understanding can make a difference between a life being taken, and one that cannot be taken. According to the Bible, Paul said, *"For I am hard-pressed between the two, having a desire to depart and be with Christ, which is far better. Nevertheless to remain in the flesh is more needful for you."* (Philippians 1:23-24) Paul had revelation, so no spiritual attack could take him before his time.

Some people accept suffering because they've convinced themselves that it is the will of God or that God is trying to teach them something. The reason for this type of reasoning is that there's no revelation. The devil has just been massaging them and harassing them. Revelation is critical. We all have witches in our lives, whether in the nuclear family or the extended family, but it is revelation that puts them under our feet to make sure they don't have any power over us. Because of false beliefs, one person may dream that they were eating at a buffet and their whole year is destroyed, while another person will have the same dream: wake up, laugh, and then move forward with life. What's the difference? Revelation.

Faith comes by hearing and hearing the Word of God. When we hear the Word of God being spoken and we have faith to open up our hearts, things change inside us. When the Word of God is being preached, you need to pay attention because you don't know when the Word that will take you into depths in the spirit will come. God allowing us to be involved in spiritual warfare is not so that we can be destroyed. If God allows His children to experience spiritual warfare, it's because He wants us to be strengthened, because battles move a person from being a child to an adult. A battle can only do that if we go into it by keeping this in our mind, "I've already won, but I'm going into this so that my strength can be enhanced."

I've shared this many times. A few years ago, I was in the office, and my body began to act strange; I talked to God, and He said, *"An attack had been launched against ministers in the land."* I asked Him what to do. He told me that the storm would be heavy, but I needed to hold on so that I would stand strong at the end of it. From that experience of a week and a few days, I learned so many things about spiritual warfare. Sometime later, I heard there was a minister in a coma during that period that I received that revelation. Suddenly, something happened to him, his health began to fail, and now he was in a coma. It was months later that I heard the testimony. After he came out of the coma, his wife of close to ten years decided she was tired of the marriage and just left. Another minister, his wife, and his children were in an accident all within that same period.

Revelation is vital. When an attack begins, I see it as another learning opportunity because I know I can never be defeated. I go into every battle with an understanding that when it is over, I will have learned more than I knew before I entered the attack. From an IT security perspective, there is something we call a 'honeypot', where one would pretend as if there are certain valuable things that you want hackers to come after, but they don't know it's a trap. You set up a fake server with fake information and allow the hackers to go in because you want to study their techniques. That's one of the ways IT folks learn hacking techniques from hackers. Every spiritual warfare for those with revelation is a way to learn the enemy's techniques.

How does the enemy initiate spiritual warfare? He starts with temptation. Suddenly a massive urge to sin against God comes very heavily upon a person. For example, the intense thought might say, "You've been a good girl all these years, so why don't you just do this bad thing? It's not going to affect anything! Why don't you just do it?" The urge comes on very strong and seems like it came out of nowhere, but all the enemy was looking for was for you to step out of grace so he could attack you.

There is a huge difference between a spiritual attack and being tested by God. Spiritual warfare and attacks originate from the devil, but a test originates from God. When God tested Abraham, it had nothing to do with the devil. God wanted to know if Abraham really loved him. It was His own idea. When God tests an individual, His intention is for that individual to pass the test; a spiritual attack is from the devil and is designed with the intention for the individual to fail. When an individual passes a test from God, the individual is uplifted, while spiritual warfare is designed to kill, steal, and destroy valuables from a person's life.

As believers, we have been designed to win every battle we fight so we must always engage in spiritual warfare from a place of strength and victory.

2

Spiritual Authority

We cannot cover everything about spiritual authority in this one chapter, but you can refer to the book I wrote on that topic, titled "The Blessings from Being Under Spiritual Authority." I encourage you to get this book and gain more understanding. Spiritual authority is one of those concepts that is well known in certain circles but not as well understood in those circles.

A spiritual authority is 'who' or 'what' we allow to control us. I used to hate the word 'control' until I started learning about being under authority. The truth is, whether you hate it or not, something is controlling you. We're all being controlled by something or someone. The difference between God and the devil in this area of spiritual authority is that God announces that he wants your submission openly. In contrast, the devil hides in the shadows and tries to take a person's will from them.

For some people, the devil controls them through fear. Every step they take is born out of fear, so that is their spiritual authority, the spirit of fear. Before the individual does anything, they will consult with fear to determine which direction to go. Fear would then say, "This is the path of least resistance. Go in that direction," and that is where they will go. They do not consult with people because fear says, "Don't talk." They've never shared a testimony of what God has done because fear says, "If you stand up there, you will fall, and people will laugh at you."

If you're unsure who has authority over you, watch out for who or what you obey because 'that' is your spiritual authority. The Lord said to me many years ago that "*he who tries to lead without being led will mislead others and be misled.*" For some, being led is only a reactive step after other methods have failed, but it is important to be proactive. In the basic leadership class at CCCG, we talked about leadership, and I reminded the class that we are all leaders, but we're all still supposed to be followers. You must never desire to get to a point where you're just a leader. These days, when people hear the word 'follower,' they think it's a very derogatory term. We're all supposed to be leaders and followers at the very same time. No human being can be on this earth without an authority over them.

Why are we talking about spiritual authority? We're saying it so that we can consciously choose who we will obey. Salvation is an introduction to spiritual authority. The Bible says you cannot serve God and mammon at the same time. Mammon is the spirit of the love of money. So, either you allow God to control you, or you allow the love of money to control you. There are a lot of people today who have money as the dictator for every decision they make. Who they date is determined by money. The job they accept is decided by money. The program they choose to study in school is driven by money. The city they choose to settle down in is determined by money. Everything they do is dictated by money, and God has no say in it. So their spiritual authority is money even though Romans 8:14 says, *"As many as are led by the Spirit of God, they are the sons of God."*

Being under authority means submitting your will to an authority figure. Not your mind, not your emotions, and not your body, but your will. Please allow me to clarify so you understand what I'm talking about. One of the reasons why people fall into traps is because they hear a little bit of the truth, and they run with it. For example, if you read the book I wrote on this topic, I said in the beginning not to start implementing anything until you read the whole book. Otherwise, someone could read a little piece and choose to submit their whole life to anyone with the title of a Pastor, then they suffer harm and believe that the principle doesn't work.

Are there people who take advantage of other people? Absolutely. Even biological parents molest their children, but does that mean all mothers and fathers are demons? Absolutely not. Man can be divided into the spirit of the man, the soul of the man, and the body of the man. Man is a spirit, has a soul, and lives in a body. The soul is made up of the will (the decision-making faculty), the mind or intellect (the thinking aspect of man), and the emotions (the feeling aspect of man). God is not saying we should submit our emotions to an authority figure. So it has nothing to do with our feelings. He is not saying we should submit our minds to an authority figure either. The Bible says to possess our minds and to guard our hearts.

When it comes to the will, Jesus said in Luke 22:42, *"... Father, if it is Your will, take this cup away from Me; nevertheless not My will, but Yours be done."* This was Jesus showing us the way to submit to spiritual authority. He had His own mind and knew what He wanted. He wanted the cup to pass over Him. The Bible says His tears were like blood, but His will was separate from His emotions. Jesus decided that regardless of what He was thinking and feeling, He was still choosing to submit to spiritual authority, *"not My will, but [the will of my authority], be done,"* (Luke 22:42), and allowed Himself to be crucified on the cross.

An ordinary person would look at Jesus and believe He had just given up His life for nothing, but Jesus knew what He was doing. *"He who descended is also the One who ascended."* (Ephesians 4:10) If He remained alive, He would've only been known in that small part of Israel. He allowed Himself to obey the Father, and now we are calling on the name of Jesus because God gave Him a name that is above every other name, that by the mention of that name, every knee must bow, and every tongue shall confess. Being under authority has many benefits, so consider me a salesman presenting you with the benefits of spiritual authority.

As we explore some of the principles of spiritual authority, I would like you to examine this line of thinking, why is it worth talking about spiritual authority, if God gave us wisdom and common sense? If God wanted us to be robots and not make decisions for ourselves, why did He give us a mind? Being under authority has lots of benefits. So, like a salesperson, I want to present the costs and benefits of being under authority so that when you decide to make that decision, it is well-informed.

Let's talk about some of the prices we have to pay to be under authority. People will take you for a fool. They would say, "Can't you think for yourself?" That's the first thing people usually say. "Can't you use your head?" There was a lady who asked God for a partner. People convinced her that her life revolved around work and church and asked her how she would find a man. When people begin to talk like that, they want to take you away from God. They want you to explore some apps, go around, and meet people. In essence, what they were saying was that her standards and principles were too high.

She told me about it, and I told her what the Word of God says. When we spoke, she said, "Pastor, what they are saying is true. I know all the guys at church. There is nobody here that is eligible." I asked her, "Are you not being short-sighted in your thinking? It's like you have looked at every permutation and combination of what can happen. You don't know who can come to church tomorrow as a new person. You don't know." To cut a long story short, I convinced her through scripture to do things the way God wanted them done, and she obeyed. Suddenly, the person God designed for her showed up, seemingly out of nowhere, and it was 'her' that that person took notice of. Why? Because she chose to submit herself to the will of God from scripture.

There is a price to pay for submission. Everybody wants to do what they want to do. There's something in man, whether an extrovert, introvert, shy person, or outspoken person, no matter who they are, that wants to do their own will. Thus, it's a price to pay, but submission has huge benefits.

As the human head of Cornerstone Christian Church of God, becoming a Pastor was the last thing I wanted to do. My parents are Pastors. I know the commitment involved, but from before I was born, prophecies already went forth. I decided to go in a different direction by supporting the church financially. I told myself that if they needed money, I would give them money.

I wanted to be the president of The World Bank. I don't remember at what age, but I remember seeing my dad heading out to work. He was a chartered accountant working at a bank while pastoring. I asked him what he did, and he told me he was a banker. I asked him what the biggest bank in the whole world was, and he said, "The World Bank." I told him, "I want to be the president of The World Bank," and he just laughed, but he didn't know I meant what I said that day. I continued on this path, studied accounting, acquired two master's degrees, and started working at the biggest consulting company in the world. I studied the people in the position and the path they took in their careers until one day when God began to speak about some things that I did not want to hear. Eventually, I submitted to God's will for my life, and I'm now in full-time ministry as a Pastor.

When we say submitting to authority, don't think of a human being just yet. Just keep thinking about God when you hear the word 'authority' because people still make that mistake again and again. I want to ask you a question. In this nation of Canada, who is our authority? Are we submitting to the Prime Minister or the Queen, or are we submitting to the Constitution of Canada? Think about it. All these people came together and put together a document, which gives authority to every other branch of government. Therefore, if the constitution is changed today to state that we no longer pledge our allegiance to the Crown, then the Crown has no more power.

Where is the power? It's in the Constitution. Suppose the Constitution is changed because of a referendum, and the federal government wants to change from a parliamentary system of government to a federal system of government. In that case, the Prime Minister no longer has any power. Unequivocally the real power is in the Constitution. That's the book that dictates everything we do; that's what we submit to. It's the law of the land.

Being under authority is submitting firstly to the Word of God which is the Constitution of the kingdom of God, not a person. We only submit to people because the Constitution says, *"Honour your father and your mother."* (Exodus 20:12) If the Bible now said, "Hate your father and your mother," then we have to follow that, but that's not what the Bible says. I believe it will be relatively easy to be under authority when we have this understanding. Furthermore, any human being can mess up, and we're not just following men blindly.

The Word of God is our number one authority. Do you know that even the devil is under the authority of the Word of God? That's why when Jesus faced the devil in Luke 4, He said, *"For it is written,"* and the devil could not talk back. Everything in heaven and on earth follows the constitution of the Word of God. That's why the devil won't allow many people to read their Bibles. He will let them go with assumptions so they come up with their own constitutions, but they don't have the authority to do that. In Luke 22:42 Jesus said, *"Father, if Thou be willing, remove this cup from Me. Nevertheless, not My will, but Your will be done."* That's a man under authority.

John 12:49-50, *"For I have not spoken on My own authority; but the Father who sent Me gave Me a command, what I should say and what I should speak. And I know that His command is everlasting life. Therefore, whatever I speak, just as the Father has told Me, so I speak."* As a Pastor here at CCCG, I have so many ideas of topics that I would like to preach about - 20 Principles of Demonic Activities; 51 Reasons Why Heaven is Real; The 20 Ways to Identify the Beast – but I shouldn't because I am not speaking on my own authority.

Sometimes I have desires for what I want to preach every month. There are some months when I feel like talking about something different, but God gives me a theme for each month, so I have to follow that theme. Just like Jesus, what the Father says I should say is what I will say, and what the Father does not say, I should not say, I will keep to myself. I desire to prophesy and deliver words of knowledge to church attendees every single service, but God said, *"I have called you to teach people how to fish and become distributors of spiritual gifts, not just consumers."*

There are situations where you know God's will, but even though you have your desire, you still aim to desire His will even though it's not what you wanted. This is okay because what we submit to God is not our emotions first but our will. When Jesus said, *"...not My will, but Yours be done,"* (Luke 22:42) He wasn't excited about dying on the cross. I want us to understand that the devil traps many people in that idea, 'You're not happy about it, so God won't be happy about it. You should just do what you want.' Jesus was not happy. He didn't want to die. The most important thing is to just obey God. The excitement will catch up with your obedience. Even if it never catches up, it doesn't matter so long as you obey God.

You may also wonder how to honour God and be blessed by Him if you're not excited about a vision He has given you but have decided to run with it diligently. God blesses you because you obeyed Him by following His instruction. Whether you are excited or not, it doesn't matter. When God told Abraham to sacrifice Isaac, was he excited? The Bible is silent about that, but I doubt that he was excited because Abraham was a human being like us all.

God is not looking for excitement first. Obedience is better than sacrifice. Excitement is sacrifice. To obey is better than the fat of rams. Just do what He has told you to do. Jesus told a story about two sons whose father gave instructions. One said he would obey it, and the other one said he wasn't going to do it, but later, it was the one who said he wasn't going to do it that decided to do it. The one who said he would do it did not do it. So Jesus said the one who eventually obeyed was the one who pleased the father.

There are certain seeds, for example, that God has asked me to sow in the past. Some were given in tears, and there was no joy in it. We share these types of testimonies so that you will grow in understanding. I was driving and focused on thanking God for the year. Meanwhile, I had started saving money for a house I wanted to buy. I heard a voice that I initially thought was the devil that instructed me to sow $5,000, which was significant from the amount I had been saving for the house. I had been hustling to get that amount when the voice came and said, *"I want you to give this amount."*

I was trying to tell God to just receive my song of worship, but the voice came back again. When the voice came, the excitement left.

Looking back today, it was nothing in me; it was the grace of God that enabled me to obey. If I say it was me, I'll be deceiving myself. I had called my Pastor at the time and asked him if he was in the office, and he was. I told him I was coming to drop something off. Immediately, I committed myself to obeying the instruction, and I drove back to my bank. I couldn't withdraw that amount of money, and I thought it was a sign from God! Then I remembered I had a chequebook which I filled out, and I went to drop off the cheque. I gave the seed as instructed and moved on. I said to myself that in the worst-case scenario, it would just take a longer period to buy the house.

By the next year, some strange things happened, and through God's hand, I was able to buy a house. I not only bought the house, but it was fully furnished with high-quality items that I still have today. They said, "We'll leave for you the dining table with chairs and all the paintings in the house." Even the pillows, throw, sofa, leather chairs from a high-end furniture store called Finesse, and the queen-sized bed in the master bedroom were left for me. I then looked at the living room's sound system and said I wanted that too. The husband said, "Yeah, for sure!" The wife said, "Honey, what's wrong with you?" I told her to leave him alone! The husband left that too, by the way.

I moved into the house with only my clothes. People heard the testimony and were in awe. God reminded me that anyone can buy houses, but not everybody buys a house with favour attached to it. All the additional things they left behind for me in the house were worth more than $15, 000. At the end of the day, who gained from the instruction that God gave? Me. In the same year, I was privileged to do some things financially. When I look back, I wonder how I was able to do all of it with what I was earning, if not by the grace of God. It's not all the time that we are excited when an instruction comes, but what God is looking at is obedience.

God knows some things would be painful for us to do. That is what I classify as sacrificial giving. Like asking Abraham to offer Isaac. But when the Bible says, *"for God loves a cheerful giver."* (2 Corinthians 9:6-7) He is referring to regular offerings and giving. In God's eyes, the question is, "How much is what you are giving that is causing you to frown on your face?" He wasn't expecting Abraham to bring Isaac cheerfully to the altar of sacrifice. Therefore, when it comes to sacrifice, God is not saying that we will always do so cheerfully.

God knows what it is like to be disobeyed because of His experience with satan, which is why He honours obedience above all else. It's one of the reasons why the Bible says, *"Obedience is better than sacrifice."* (1 Samuel 15:22) It is impossible to be under spiritual authority without control. That is why there is no way to be under authority without humility.

Humility is needed to submit to authority. It's what makes you and I decide, "You know what, I have my mind, my will, and my emotions, but I 'choose' to lay those things at the altar." Humility enables you and me to gracefully submit our will to another. What I'm sharing has transformed my life. If not for all levels of spiritual authority, I would not be alive today.

Let's read Matthew 8:8-9; the centurion answered and said, *"Lord, I am not worthy that You should come under my roof. But only speak a word, and my servant will be healed. For I also am a man under authority, having soldiers under me. And I say to this one, 'Go,' and he goes; and to another, 'Come,' and he comes; and to my servant, 'Do this,' and he does it."* The centurion alluded to the idea that nobody can have authority if they have not submitted to authority.

POWER vs AUTHORITY

Power and authority are different. Power is good, but it always has to be generated. There are many ways to generate power, for example, fasting and prayer. The moment you stop fasting and praying, power will dissipate. If you don't pay your bills, the power company will cut your access to power over time even though there is a capacity for power. Authority functions differently. Power can never last for a lifetime, but authority can. That's why even though I accumulate power, I focus my attention on authority.

If you look at a country, for example, the military has tanks and guns to maintain law and order. The moment they don't have tanks or guns anymore is the moment they don't have power anymore. They have to keep using force to keep the people subdued. Democracy, on the other hand, is a thing of authority. We, the people, 'supposedly' voted them in and gave them authority to rule over us. In Canada, for example, even though Justin Trudeau does not personally have guns and tanks, he has authority over the army and other branches of the military. The moment we vote him out, his authority ends. Stephen Harper, the previous Canadian Prime Minister, no longer has authority over Canada because the people have withdrawn the authority they gave him to rule over Canadians.

So, that's the difference between power and authority. Now the centurion was saying, "I also am a man under authority. So because of that, I say to this one 'Go', and he goes. I say to this one 'Come', and he comes. I say to this one, 'Do this', and he does it because of the authority that I have." How did the centurion get the authority? He got it because he was under authority. One of the things I'm trusting God for you today is to understand the reason why you must never be rebellious.

What is Rebellion? Sadly, in some churches, if the Pastor looks at an item and says, "I think this should be here," and you suggest, "No,

Pastor. Why don't we put it like this," it is interpreted as you being rebellious. That makes no sense at all. That's not what I'm talking about. As I stated earlier, being under spiritual authority does not mean you are submitting your mind; your mind should be working. Some people cannot be themselves around their human authority. That's not what I'm talking about either. That's bondage.

Apostle John was resting on the bosom of Jesus. He was that close to Jesus, but he was still submitted to Him. Your emotional life can be alive; your mind can be alive; you can think differently from your human authority and still be under authority. That's how you get the most value because you still retain your individuality despite submitting to a human authority. When you are under authority, 'you' have authority. I aim for authority and want to remain in it because I've realized that even though fasting is good, there's a limit.

Prayer is good, but it is impossible to pray all the time, 365 days a year. I don't mean praying in the spirit, because the Bible says, *"pray without ceasing."* (I Thessalonians 5:17) I attempt to do that, so I'm not talking about that. I'm talking about actively praying with our mouths, where you can't eat or go anywhere, and you can't even preach because your mouth is just moving all the time! It's impossible to pray in that manner past a particular period of time. I have heard of people who have prayed for 36 hours straight. Most likely, that's under the power of the Holy Ghost. Even Paul, in the Bible, encouraged the church to pray for him because he got to a point where he had to sleep - his body got tired. In essence, he was saying, "I've seen visions of the third heavens, and you are not as powerful as me, but still pray for me."

There are certain levels of power that we cannot generate by our prayers alone. In Ephesians 6, the Bible talks about different categories of demons: principalities, powers, rulers of darkness, and hosts of wickedness in heavenly places. When you call a group 'powers', you know that they specialize in power, but authority would make a person reign over people with power; this is the way of authority.

I'll give you evidence from scripture. The Bible never told us that Elisha did 40 days of fasting and prayer to get power, but the Bible said Elisha poured water on the hands of Elijah, which means Elisha served Elijah. As a result of that, he entered into authority over the land through service. He wasn't the only prophet in the land. The Bible said that as they moved from Bethel to Jordan and from Jordan to different places, there were sons of the prophets of different places who had the word of knowledge.

They knew Elijah was going to die, so they were walking in the gifts of the Spirit, but only Elisha – because of his service – got to a point where he got a double portion. Elijah said, "Stay here. I'm going there," but Elisha said, "No, no, no. I'm going with you. I will keep serving you. You cannot chase me away." That's being under authority. There are many ideas the devil has put into people's hearts and minds to 'be your own boss. You can do your own thing!' Those things will only take you so far.

THE STAGES OF RELATING TO HUMAN SPIRITUAL AUTHORITY

There are three levels: **Dependence, Independence,** and **Interdependence.**

Dependence

The first level is where you are dependent. You always need someone's help to do everything, like a newborn baby. You have to breastfeed the baby. The baby cannot make lasagna or other delicious meals. It can't do things on its own.

Independence

Independence is the second level of development. Here, the baby grows to become independent, where they can whip up a meal themselves and begin to have friends.

Interdependence

Now, the third level is interdependence, which we should aim to achieve - where even though you can be independent - you choose to connect with another independent person to achieve a joint purpose. Anybody could be the Pastor of this great church if they are submitted to God and He chose them to do it. He chose me to do it, which is why I'm in this position as the Pastor, not because I'm the best. Certain giftings come with the office of being in authority so that I can function effectively. The leaders that God has chosen in this Ministry are anointed in their own right, but they cannot say, "Why don't we all come together and pick the theme of the year for the church?" It's impossible. Anything like that is from the devil because it is my responsibility as the authority. God can speak to you regarding your life and your family, but the church? No. So interdependence is bringing all our individual gifts together to achieve God's purpose and vision.

Someone asked me, "How come certain things only happen when you come on the stage?" And I explained that people could be spiritual in their own right, but God does not violate authority except if the person He puts on top has failed numerous times, like Saul. He does not like disorder or chaos. That's why even when a system is no longer working, God can keep it because He is building something different as a replacement. He can keep it there for another 20, 40, or 60 years because He has another plan. There are some denominations that you may think that God should scatter, but He's saying, "No, no, no." He's considering some innocent people who might be affected. He believes in order.

What are the different authorities we ought to submit to? I'll explain this in the order of the hierarchy God has established.

THE HIERARCHY OF SPIRITUAL AUTHORITY

THE WORD OF GOD

This is not the word of man. This is the number one authority that a child of God must submit to. For example, suppose someone offends you, and you don't feel like forgiving. In that case, you can remember that the Bible says, *"Forgive,"* and then you submit to that Word and forgive. Even if you don't feel like it, and they did not apologize, you must still forgive. Even if they said, "Me? I will never say I'm sorry", but because of the Bible, you will say, "You know what, I forgive you, even though you don't deserve it."

In Matthew 28:18, Jesus said, *"...all authority in heaven and on earth has been given to me."* Since Jesus is the Word, all authority has been put in the Word.

THE HOLY SPIRIT

Romans 8:14 says, *"As many as are led by the Spirit of God they are the sons (and the daughters) of God,"* therefore, the Holy Spirit has the right to lead us. How?

Acts 13:1-3 reads, *"Now in the church that was at Antioch there were certain prophets and teachers: Barnabas, Simeon who was called Niger, Lucius of Cyrene, Manaen who had been brought up with Herod the tetrarch, and Saul. As they ministered to the Lord and fasted, the Holy Spirit said, "Now separate to Me Barnabas and Saul for the work to which I have called them." Then, having fasted and prayed, and laid hands on them, they sent them away."* Even if Paul and Barnabas may have heard from the Holy Spirit themselves, God will still confirm it to their spiritual authority so they can be blessed.

Whether or not their authority receives and accepts that word is a different case entirely. Either way, there has to be an agreement. Furthermore, if we know that the Holy Spirit speaks, we must explore 'how' the Holy Spirit speaks. Many people miss out on hearing from God because they do not allow God to determine how He wants to speak to them. The Holy Spirit can speak through either what we hear, see, or perceive, and sometimes a mixture of all these. In my experience, perception is where most people face the biggest challenge, primarily because many people do not meditate as much as they should.

I've shared this example before. A particular woman in another ministry said the Holy Spirit told her that a particular man (who was someone else's husband) was her husband, and so because the kingdom of God suffers violence and the violent takes it by force, she had to take the man by force. You and I know that would never have been the Holy Spirit.

The Bible says, "The Spirit of God will take from what is Mine and give unto you." The Holy Spirit will only take the Word of God and give that to us. So the Holy Spirit will NOT go against God's Word when communicating God's will to us. That's why we need to be in the Word of God to know what the Bible is saying. When I started hearing the voice of God, it was while I was reading the Bible. Not while I was praying or sitting in silence but when I was reading the Bible. If you want to connect with the prophetic, read the Bible. That's one of the fastest ways to prophetic giftings. Read the Bible. The Bible is a sure word of prophecy.

HUMAN AUTHORITY

In 1 Peter 5:5, we see different ways of submission: *"Likewise you younger people, submit yourselves to your elders,"* and *"all of you be submissive to one another."* Can you imagine a scenario in an organization where the CEO says everybody should go right, but your immediate team leader says everybody should go left? If a team member is wise, who should they listen to? If they go with the team leader, they would lose their job! They should listen to the CEO because that's the one who has the authority. When people don't know how to hear from the CEO, they are stuck listening to team leaders only and then go astray.

I saw a very heart-wrenching video many years ago. Some supposed Christians were out in a field, and cameras were recording them while eating grass because a supposed man of God told them that the spirit said they should eat grass. Those observing asked one of the individuals eating how the grass tasted, and they said, "Macaroni pasta. Tastes like macaroni pasta." I saw the woman's eyes, and her eyes looked like she was demonized. As I watched, my heart was breaking, and I wanted to speak against whoever that man was, but God said, *"No, no, no. Even the people themselves are at fault. It's not just the Pastor. Don't they have a Bible to read?"* If they read their Bibles, they won't fall into a trap like that. But they're susceptible to deception because they don't read the Word.

There's a ministry in Kenya that is called "Breast and Honey Ministries". So to get a miracle, the Pastor would suck the breast of the person. Are there people who attend the ministry? Yes. People are there because they don't read their Bibles. All of these result from a desperate search for miracles because they don't read their Bibles. So who is to blame? Both parties are to blame. This is why we emphasize the authority of the Word. The primary authority is the Word of God, *"And you shall know the truth, and the truth shall make you free."* (John 8:32)

I was close to someone I used to Pastor before they relocated. The individual told me they went to a particular church and met a strange Pastor. She told the Pastor that she needed deliverance. The man looked at her and prayed. Then he said, "God said there has to be intercourse, a spiritual interaction." She told him she needed to think about it. She was desperate, but she went home. Thank God she went to talk to a sensible Christian. That is absolute nonsense and against the Word of God.

The Word of God is the authority. In another instance, someone went to a man of God and said, "God said I should tell you that you should sow this amount of money into my life. The Pastor said, "No. God has not told me anything." The man was insistent that God had told him to tell the Pastor this, but the Pastor said, "I just finished speaking to God now. If He wants to tell me that, He will tell me Himself."

Let me break this down for us to understand. God can tell us that He wants someone to sow a seed. He can tell me to tell you to sow a seed, but hardly would He tell me to tell you the amount of money you should sow. When the devil came to test Jesus, he told Him that He should jump, and then he quoted Psalm 91, "He will cause His angels to keep charge over you." Jesus was wiser; He knew that the devil was quoting that scripture incorrectly, and so, in response, Jesus quoted, "You shall not tempt the Lord your God " (Matthew 4:7) Yes, He will cause His angels to keep charge over me, but that's if I mistakenly fall, not when I intentionally jump. That is intentional suicide, and God will not override any human being's will. He'll say, "Maybe they're tired of living. Angels, don't go." But if someone pushed the person, He would cause angels to keep charge over them.

We need to be careful. Read the Word. Where the Word is missing, the Spirit will fill in the blanks. And where the Word is missing and the Spirit of God is missing because of our inability to connect, our human authorities will fill in the blanks. When we do things the way God wants them done, we can never miss anything God has to say. There is nothing in God that God wants to tell me today that I will miss. If I don't hear it directly, I'm connected with the right people, and so the information will flow by the grace of God. There are blessings of being under spiritual authority. Within the realm of human authorities, we have three categories:

1. **Spiritual Authorities - The Church**
2. **Biological - Your Parents**
3. **Government Authorities**

Spiritual Authorities – The Church

The Bible clearly shows that Jesus Christ owns and is the head of the church. In Matthew 16:18, Jesus said, "*I will build My church, and the gates of Hades shall not prevail against it.*" Apostle Paul also asserted that "*Christ is head of the church*" in teaching about marriage and the husband's role in the home (Ephesians 5:23).

The kingdom of God on the earth is also domiciled in the church. We are told in Acts 2:42 that from the early days of the church, the disciples (Christians) submitted themselves to the Apostles' doctrine. The early church understood that they had to be governed by the leadership instituted by the Holy Spirit. A doctrine is simply the interpretation of scripture adopted by a congregation. Just like every family has a right to determine where to place their furnishings within their home, a church government has a right to decide how to govern the church in line with their biblical understanding. In essence, church denominations are a product of different apostles' doctrines from different interpretations of scripture. While some might think this is a problem, this is actually by design.

Every Christian church is, by design, supposed to look different, just like each human being looks different even when they come from the same family. Apostle Paul understood this principle as reflected in his confidence in setting up systems for the assemblies he presided over (1 Corinthians 11). While every individual is made up of the same primary components like blood, water, kidneys, heart, etc., we do not all look the same. There is strength in our diversity, which helps preserve us from generation to generation. Christians must understand that the Holy Spirit does not determine everything within an assembly. The hope is that those responsible for leading assemblies rely on the word of God and the Holy Spirit as much as possible in determining how the assembly they preside over should be structured and governed.

Every believer ought to be under the authority of Jesus Christ within a church. No matter who you are and the anointing you carry, you must be a part of a local church and be submitted to Christ there. Like in the natural realm, every individual must be a citizen of at least one nation to perform everyday functions. This concept was validated by how the authority of the church preserved Apostle Peter's life in Acts 12.

One kingdom (the earthly government) captured Apostle James. It killed him because another kingdom (the church) did not rise to pray. When Apostle Peter was arrested and going to be killed, however, the church rose to pray and, in essence, challenged the earthly government and prevailed. Apostle Peter was anointed as an individual, but his anointing did not preserve him against the governance system. This exemplifies the need for every individual to be submitted to Jesus Christ's authority within a local church. Perhaps the church has needlessly lost apostles, evangelists, teachers, prophets, pastors, missionaries, etc. because they did not see the need to submit themselves to the authority of the church.

The only authority empowered to commission disciples into ministry work is the church. The church as a whole or as represented by its God-ordained leaders are the only ones authorized to commission people into service. In Acts 13, even though God called Paul and Barnabas to serve, the church leadership's representatives laid hands on them to authorize them to act on behalf of the church. Just like in a democratic governance system, you can win an election (similar to being called by God), but until you are sworn in (similar to being ordained), you are not authorized to govern.

Biological – Your Parents

Whether or not I am someone's spiritual authority and whether I'm older than them or younger than them, it doesn't matter; once I get to a person's home, I submit to the authority of that home. I can never talk to a man's wife or give instructions without the husband's permission. I would never do that because if I did, I would be violating authority and violating scriptures.

I am not saying that a man is better than a woman, but it is a matter of principles. If a wife comes to me, even for a meeting, and says, "Oh, this is what my husband is doing," I would never agree that the husband made a mistake in front of her. Instead, I would tell her what she can do to get what she wants, according to scripture. Once I get a chance to meet with the husband, I'll never say, "Why did you do that? What's wrong with you? How can you behave like this?" in the presence of the wife. That's why many of the women feel like I let their husbands off so easily, but they do not fully understand the principle of authority. You don't scold an elder in front of the people they're leading; you're breaking scriptures and are giving the followers permission and ammunition to go against them. In the Old Testament, God said that if a wife were to make a vow (and God does not joke with vows) and their husband hears about the vow, the husband has the authority to cancel that vow.

Even though both parents are authorities over a child, if a father curses a child, that child will remain cursed, no matter what the mother does, unless an authority higher than the father cancels that curse. An example of this in scripture is when Jacob cursed his older children on his deathbed and subjected them to their younger siblings because they acted against Jacob's wishes after the incident with their sister. However, when you fast forward to the time of Moses, the Levites received the responsibility of the priestly office because they chose to stand with God and Moses when the Israelites started worshipping idols. Due to the authority that Moses possessed, Jacob's curse over Levi was cancelled.

Government Authorities

Romans 12 tells us that we should obey those who rule over us. So God expects us to abide by the speed limit, for example, because the government is the one who put that there. You can't say, "Oh, I know that the speed limit is 50, but I just feel like it should be 60, so I feel led to drive at 60." If I feel led to go past the speed limit, the police officer would also feel led to give me a ticket!

Everywhere you are, there is an authority that God has ordained for you to succeed; you need to submit to the relevant authorities. When I enter a workplace with a new contract, I scan to locate the authority there and submit myself. Some people want to get promoted, but in their hearts, they don't submit to their boss. I can assure you it will not happen because you're breaking spiritual principles. Even if your boss desires to promote you because you are violating principles, they will think, "No, no, no. This is not a good idea for us." I'm not talking about eye service; if you submit to them in your heart, nobody can limit your rising!

We like to quote scripture in Ephesians 6:1-4, *"Children, submit to your parents... honor your father and mother."* Fantastic! But Verse 4 says,

"...fathers, do not provoke your children to wrath..." The way some people lead makes it difficult for people not to be rebellious because they don't allow people to contribute. Everything is, "God said," even when He didn't, and there's no room for people to come and contribute and add their own creativity. Either way, if a leader now comes and says, "This is what it is," anybody that goes against it is rebellious.

Submission to authority is what the Bible says we should do, regardless of who the authority is. Let's say the person in authority says, "I want it to be here," and I think it is better somewhere else; then I will say politely, "Sir (or ma'am), I think it will be better here because of such and such reason." If the person says, "Uh, thanks for your opinion, but I think that is silly, so I'd like it to be placed here," I will then say, "Okay, I will move it there," even if I disagree with it. I will keep my opinion to myself. My mind will still believe that my option was better, but my will has decided to put it *here*. So when I get to a place where I have my own authority, I can now place things where I want them unless God gives me revelation on why my authority had made that decision.

There are some things about authority that you should understand so that you can enjoy yourself while being under authority. There are different aspects of our lives, and God has designed different authorities to take charge of those different areas. Many people say, 'my spiritual father' or 'my spiritual mother,' and spiritual this and that. Let me explain; Paul said that you can have many teachers, but you can only have one father. Many human authorities can cover different aspects of a person's life. But there must be one authority that oversees all of them.

That's where a spiritual father or mother comes in, and that's what Paul was trying to say; you can have only one father, but it can be a mother as well. You can have one spiritual father or mother but many teachers. When you send your child to school, one teacher teaches the child mathematics, another English, another one teaches them physical education, social studies, and so on. They also participate in different activities, but when they come home, the child is fully under your authority.

As parents, we have the right to overrule anything that any of their other teachers have said. Without this understanding, people will get confused. They submit to all kinds of people without an understanding of the principles governing submission to human authority. For example, let's say, a person wants to get married, they've prayed about it, and now they want to get confirmation. They then go to authority number one who says it's a yes; they go to authority number two who says it's a maybe; authority number three says it's a capital 'NO'; and finally, authority number 4 says it's a yes. Now, which one should they follow, especially if the individual has placed them all on the same authority level? No one!

That's why Paul said you could have many teachers, and I call teachers mentors. God is the one who designs those things. Just like you've never selected your biological parents, He is the one who chooses spiritual parents. If you're sensitive, He is the one who orchestrates the connection. When you see them, you will know that there is a connection because their words go directly into your heart.

Some identified their spiritual authority through visitations in their dreams and visions. God meets everybody at their own level because some people need a lot of proof to understand. Those are just some examples. Many times, like in my case, the spiritual parents might not necessarily be the biological parent; however, in some cases, the biological parent can be the spiritual parent as well. It depends on their level of authority in the spirit.

BLESSINGS OF BEING UNDER SPIRITUAL AUTHORITY

SPIRITUAL COVERING

That is why I said that being under spiritual authority has saved my life. We were having a photo shoot some time ago, and the social media team at CCCG asked me which book I had written was my favourite; I told them that I liked "A Disciplined Life," but my favourite is, "The Blessings of Being Under Spiritual Authority" because Divine covering can save a person's life.

Jesus told Peter that the devil wanted to sift him as wheat, but He had prayed that Peter's faith would not fail. If you are truly under spiritual authority, there is no way that the authority would not be aware of things in the spirit concerning you; and I am talking about a real authority that is submitted to God. They might not properly understand what they are hearing or seeing, but there is no way they would not be notified. Even biological parents who are maybe not as spiritual can testify that they can sense when something is off with their child; how much more spiritual parents?

For example, sometimes I would be driving, and I would think of a church member or someone that I am privileged to be an authority over. The thought of them would come, and if I begin to feel irritated by them, I would know that they are under attack. If I think of them and there is a feeling of excitement and love, and I am just happy and smiling, I know God is about to bless them with favour. And those are just two examples out of so many other ways.

Let us touch on perception. Perception is very broad in scope. You can tell when the enemy is attacking a person because they lose their colour, shine, and attractiveness. In some cases, for example, if there is a heightened state of demonic activity, the person will carry a certain type of stench. A spiritually sensitive person would know that there is something off with that person. I was in prayer once, and I saw one of my daughters, and she appeared blind with someone leading her. I woke up, and I declared, "No, never!" I stood against it, and I moved on. That person would never hear about that dream from me because I don't share bad news. That is no longer bad news; it's now good news! Life goes on. It is important to note that no one should provide spiritual covering for someone else if they themselves are not covered. That is not authority.

Only a person with authority can give an inheritance to those under their authority, and the inheritance is in the blessings that the authority speaks over that person. And what do I mean by blessings? Any Tom, Dick, and Harry can say "God bless you", but when someone in authority, that you submit to, says "God bless you", and you receive it, something in your life will change for the better. I've seen it happen again and again too many times!

HONOUR

When we submit to authority, we are also honoured. When Jesus was going to ride triumphantly into Jerusalem, He told his disciples to look for a Colt, that is, a baby donkey that had never been ridden before. Normally, a donkey would not be walking, and people would throw their clothes on the donkey. But because Jesus was now sitting on the donkey, the same honour that was given to Jesus was also given to the donkey He was riding. The same honour given to the president of a nation is the same honour given to the ambassador of that nation because when they appear there, they appear in the name of the president they represent.

When the US ambassador to Canada shows up to a college or a cottage, they will be received as if they are receiving the president because that person comes with the authority of the United States government. This is why when Elisha sent one of the sons of the prophet to anoint Jehu, Jehu allowed him because he was coming in the name of Elisha, who was the prophet over the land. So when you are under authority, the honour that is given to your authority will be given to you too. One way I know people who don't submit to authority is that they're usually dishonoured.

DIVINE DIRECTION

A few years ago, there was a guy I am still privileged to have authority over. Many years ago, before Cornerstone started, he charged at me in anger and just began to vent. He was wondering why God wasn't answering his questions. I was just looking at him. I asked myself, "Who is this guy talking about?" and so I asked him if he was talking about God! He said he was fasting, praying, and asking God simple questions, but no answer was coming.

As I watched him, God spoke to me, and this was how I got this revelation I'm about to share; God said, *"No matter how spiritual you are; I will never tell you everything about your own life. Otherwise, there would be no need for you to be under human authority."* Immediately I heard that, I started smiling. He asked me why I was smiling. I didn't get offended by his question because if he could be rude to God, why wouldn't he be rude to me? I asked him what question he was even asking to start with. He told me calmly this time and I laughed even more. I told him that a few days prior, I was eating jollof rice and chicken, and while I was eating, the same answer he was asking God for was told to me, and I didn't even ask for it. God just told me. He got even angrier and said, "Why is God telling you, but I'm praying, and He's not telling me?"

I then understood what God was saying. If God tells us everything about our lives, we would never see the need to submit to anybody.

If you tried to submit, it would not be genuine. When we are under authority, God sends the word we need. It is our responsibility to seek the will of God. You can ask Him first, but He didn't tell you the answers would be given to you directly.

I remember when Cornerstone was about to start, and God gave me all the information, including the name of the church. It sounded so good to me, and I thought the name would already have been taken. Nigeria alone has the name of every church so, in my mind, I thought that Cornerstone Christian Church Of God was already taken. I went online and looked all over the world, but there was no record that the name was taken.

I had been asking the Lord when we should have our first service, but I didn't get any answer. My dad came to visit in October 2012. One morning, he woke up early and knocked on my door. He asked if he could come into my room, and then asked if I had my calendar. He pointed to December 2014 and asked me what day the first Sunday was. I replied that it was the 7th, and he said that was the first service of the ministry; it was to start on December 7th, 2014. He explained the significance of that date, saying that seven represents perfection, and he elaborated on some other details. I weighed it with everything else God had told me because I needed to test all spirits. He instructed me to fast and pray for three months, and have Bible studies in the same period. After that, the ministry would start. The 7th aligned with everything God had said, but before that, I had been praying and asking when it would happen. He chose to answer me that way, even though my biological father did not even know I was seeking that information.

Though this building is double the size of the church he Pastors in Nigeria, I recognize that he is an authority over me. It has never entered my mind that I am superior to him. If such a thought were to enter my mind, I would consider it to be a demonic thought and would fight against it. This struggle frequently happens to many people. We are all spiritual people, but there will come a time when we will pray about something, and it will not come to pass.

Being under authority is a matter of the heart; it is not about putting on a show for others. God knows the heart of each person. Occasionally, He will reveal the hearts of others to us, but most of the time, He sees what we do not.

A few years ago, I noticed a pattern. When I ministered to some people, the Spirit of God would move through me, and words would come to me through the Holy Spirit's inspiration. However, when I sat with others, it felt like the heavens had closed, and nothing flowed. I wondered why this was happening, and I thought it was because I hadn't prayed enough. I am sharing this information to help us understand that this is leadership. One day, the Lord spoke to me, saying that the difference is that some people have submitted to the grace of God on my life while others have not.

The Bible says that, like water, the heart of man responds to another man's heart. It is a matter of the heart, so you may not always know why you feel a certain way. You might think of me and become angry or look at my shoes and feel upset. I feel your pain. That is the work of the devil. The enemy is targeting your heart and your connection with others. I cannot tell you how many times I have dreamed of my spiritual father chasing me and saying things that would make me angry. I would wake up and say, "Devil, really?" Then I would text my spiritual father to tell him I loved him. That response puts the nail in the coffin. The devil is a liar.

WHAT HUMAN SPIRITUAL AUTHORITY IS NOT

AN INABILITY:
TO SPEAK YOUR MIND WITH RESPECT

You are not in bondage when you are under authority. Where the Spirit of God is, there is liberty and freedom. If you feel there is bondage and the authority is God-ordained, you need to check to ensure that you are understanding things correctly and not relying on your culture. Being under authority should never mean that you cannot express your opinion with respect.

A REPLACEMENT FOR GOD

God is a jealous God, and nobody should take His place. If someone comes to me and asks for direction, and I know they have not gone to God in prayer, I will send them back to God. No matter how much I know, I will not say anything. Typically, I would instruct the individual to pray, or go on a retreat, and come back if needed. Most of the time, they might ask someone else to tell them.

Any direction from any authority must conform to the will of God and must be in alignment with the Word of God. If they say, "I know the Bible says that, but I am telling you otherwise," You should respond and say, "Thank you very much, I really appreciate it, but I am going to follow what the Bible says."

AN INABILITY: TO THINK

As stated previously, being under spiritual authority doesn't mean a loss in your ability to think. When you submit to authority, your mind is not shut down. You can think for yourself and seek counsel to validate or correct your way of thinking. So you are not submitting your mind but your will.

Why is it possible for an individual police officer to stop you when you are driving beyond the speed limit? One of the main reasons why people, even though they have power and are anointed, are still trapped and subdued is because of the authority they're under. There is something the kingdom of God and even the kingdom of darkness akin to. They're likened to the military with a chain of command. Once you understand that concept it will be very easy for all of us to be under authority. That's the way it works.

In every kingdom, each office has areas that they are in charge of, and they have the authority to fulfil the obligations of that office. When we talk about spiritual authority, those are offices with roles and responsibilities. For every responsibility in the kingdom, some resources have been assigned to fulfil that responsibility.

That's the whole idea of authority. God gives power mainly domiciled in positions. Anybody outside the chain of command that seems to have power is just temporary. For example, He has put me in the position of a Pastor. To fulfill that calling, even without fasting and prayer, I would still be a blessing to people as I make myself available for God's use. I may not be a blessing to myself, but I will still be a blessing to people. That's why when Eli, for example, was out of line with God, he could still be a blessing to Hannah when she needed it. Remember, he had gone astray already, and God was already looking for how to replace him. While raising Samuel, Eli was still in the position of a high priest and was still able to minister to people who came to Shiloh.

The authority is domiciled in the position, and the devil knows, so he targets positions. If he can get just his people into positions, he can get what comes with the position and the people they rule over. That is the whole idea around principalities and powers. That's why they target rulers and people in positions of authority. It's like buy one, get many for free. If the enemy can put someone that compromises the mayor, the whole of Edmonton will be under the sway of the enemy. It's as simple as that. That's why the Lord told me that whoever can change a system is way more powerful than the one that makes people fall down under that anointing.

I thank God for physical displays of power, but my focus is on continually growing in authority to change systems. That is the real issue. Whoever can get things written in the policies and laws that everybody has to follow, regardless of their faith, has real power. That is why the enemy targets the positions. Fathers run a position of authority. When the devil compromises them, they can speak words over all those under their domain and lead them into destruction if they choose to. That's why the whole concept of spiritual authority is important. The best way to operate is in authority. God helps every one of us to be perfectly aligned to His chain of command.

As I mentioned in the book, "The Blessings of Being Under Spiritual Authority," being under spiritual authority is a blessing from God to ensure that you are aligned with His will. Nobody has real authority if they're not under God's authority. When you are perfectly aligned with someone under God's authority, as Paul said, you would know that no harm can successfully overpower you or bring you down. It is absolutely impossible.

I saw a scene where people tried to rescue a drowning person from the sea. There was a human chain in which some people went as deep as they could, and they were connected person by person to those far away from the water. Nobody drowned as long as they kept holding each other in that chain. This allowed them to rescue the people they needed to rescue. That's one of the reasons why I know that no devil can kill me before my time. They can keep trying but I know it will never happen, no matter who you are.

Someone once said that God told her that whenever her faith is not working, she should tap into the faith of her spiritual father, and I just smiled because God was trying to help her. I remember when my spiritual father was on a 21-day fast, and after praying for those days, he called, and every benefit of those prayers was passed to me. When you are under spiritual authority, you can benefit from someone else's labour. The devil does not tell you that, though. All he says is that someone is trying to control your life. Who has time to control everyone's lives? With my responsibilities, I don't have time to control people's lives. It is a privilege even to see someone still concerned about your situation to help you and give you advice. But the devil just tells you that they're trying to control you.

Revelation is good, and it will put you at ease. God said to me one day that whenever someone comes and asks me to mentor them, it's more responsibility. This is because I am giving way more and will always give more than I receive from them. That's the way it will always be. A child can decide to bless the parents here and there, but you can never equate what the parent has done for the child to what the child is privileged to do for the parent. How can you repay your mother for carrying you for nine months in the womb? All the morning sickness in the afternoon and at night. You can never! Once you get that revelation, you'll be at peace. There are blessings in being under spiritual authority.

3

Humility

Matthew 18:4 says, *"Therefore, whoever humbles himself as this little child is the greatest in the kingdom of heaven."* Not *shall* be the greatest, but *is* the greatest. It is very profound. Not whoever 'God' humbles, but whoever humbles 'themselves.' Until we humble ourselves, greatness will never emerge. The moment we get the revelation that humility is the best route to take in every situation, greatness has already begun. The rest are just manifestations. In the kingdom of God, you are a great person.

GREATNESS IN THE KINGDOM OF GOD

Greatness in the kingdom of heaven is being able to manifest heaven wherever we go. That is a tall order for an average person. This means we will do what Jesus would have done whenever we show up. The Bible gives us the benchmark for humbling ourselves: as a little child, not as our father or mother. We do not know the age of the child Jesus was referring to. Greatness in the kingdom of heaven is also what Paul experienced. When the sons of Sceva tried to perform an exorcism on a particular demon-possessed man, the demons responded, *"Jesus I know, Paul I know, but who are you?"* (Acts 19:11-17) They simply said, " Your name is not registered in heaven as anybody great in the kingdom of God." Greatness is when demons know who we are and recognize us as an authority. We do not have to stand on a stage to be in authority.

There are some things that challenged me from the scriptures, and there are still some things that challenge me today. When Jesus was teaching in the temple, demons began to manifest and said, *"What do you want with us, Son of God?"* they shouted. *"Have you come here to torture us before the appointed time?"* (Matthew 8:29) And Jesus rebuked them and told them to keep quiet. That is greatness in the kingdom of heaven. Many of us have experienced these things, but perhaps we did not know what was happening. It is not about money or certain things that the world has told us to define as success; it is authority, and this is what I am personally striving towards by the grace of God.

In the case of Abraham, God wanted to destroy Sodom and Gomorrah, and He asked Himself why He would want to do something like this without telling Abraham. Greatness also means that God cannot do certain things in the places where we are located without letting us know. It is almost like God is hindered and cannot take a step without letting us know what He wants to do in our domain. When Don Iverson was contesting in the last municipal election, I realized I had a right to ask certain questions. The Holy Spirit began to tell me that this person would win by 80%. We want to reach a point where God can reveal even the message our Pastor will preach to us. God gives us these revelations not so that we can broadcast them as little children would but simply because He wants us to know. This is greatness in the kingdom of heaven.

The Bible states that Enoch was taken by God, and someone said that God enjoyed their fellowship so much that He took him to heaven with Him rather than wasting transport fare from heaven to earth. Personally, I desire such a close relationship with God. For married people, imagine coming home and finding out that your spouse just bought a new house without informing you and then announcing that you are moving the next day. You would have wanted to have that information and made the decisions together. Again, if your spouse suddenly changed jobs and you found out they had made the decision three months ago without informing you, you would feel like you weren't truly their partner.

THE HUMILITY OF MOSES

The Bible says that Moses was the meekest person or one of the meekest people on the face of the earth. Why was Moses described as this? Moses was a very great man; to be meek means humble, Moses was known as one of the most humble men, but why was that so? Can you imagine a mere human being able to part the Red Sea? Just try to picture it - you stand in front of a swimming pool, raise your hand, and suddenly, the water separates! It's not something easy to experience, believe me. When we talk about pride, it is often referred to as having a swollen head, and this is true. However, Moses, despite having the power to destroy his enemies, chose not to fight back, even when people came against him. This is one reason why he was considered the humblest man on earth. He possessed immense spiritual power, greater than any other man at that time.

Another reason why Moses was humble was that he obeyed every commandment from God. Just because one has the power to do something does not mean God wants them to do it. Moses obeyed when God told him to go back to Egypt, even though his life was in danger. It was a risky journey, but he went ahead anyway because God had instructed him to do so. This is humility.

I may not be at Moses' level, but I have experienced what it feels like when someone younger in the faith tries to challenge you, thinking that they can defeat you. It's like having a little child hitting you, and even though you have the power to kick them, you know that you cannot do that. All you can do is keep praying in the spirit while they keep hitting you. Imagine being at Moses' level and facing challenges from Mariam and Aaron, who were older, and his siblings. They were not happy with his choice of an Ethiopian wife, but Moses said nothing. God confronted them and reminded them of who they were talking about. From this, I learned never to fight anyone who attacks me personally. However, if someone were to attack the people God has placed under my care, I would fight for them. If anyone touches my wife, they are as good as dead. That's when you see that being gentle is not always appropriate. I only need to speak one word, and the person will be gone, which can mean many things.

I recall signing a contract when a lady high up in the chain of command started firing contractors. She was the next manager above my city manager, and people were afraid of her. I prayed to God and asked if it was time for me to leave, but He told me to stay. The next thing I knew, the woman was fired, and the idea of firing contractors ended. I knew that if I was still there, it meant that she couldn't be there. The organization went through a merger, new branches were created, and the woman was kicked out.

God has the power to empower us and our imagination, but we must make the conscious decision not to use this power to enrich ourselves. Instead, we must recognize that God is the one who can benefit us directly. We can learn from Moses, who operated at this level of understanding, but it all begins with revelation. Once we have this understanding, we can apply it in our daily lives. For example, when people dishonour us, we should assess ourselves first to ensure that we are in right standing with God. If we are, then we should assume that they do not know better and forgive them, allowing God to take us to higher levels.

Some people make a lot of noise about their giving, but the amount they give is not proportional to the noise they make. On the other hand, some people give generously without making any noise about it. For instance, a family received a tax refund of $29,000, and God instructed them to sow it all into the church, which they did without even informing me. They just sowed it into the church because God instructed them to do that. These people had plans to buy a house, so when it was time to buy a house, they had no down payment. If they had mentioned it to me, I would have told them to hold on to the money first and reconfirm again!

When it was time to buy a house, God told them to talk to me, so I advised them to look for the house even though they had no down payment. They saw one that was quite expensive, and I told them to purchase it. They asked me what they should do, and I responded that I didn't know yet. However, I advised them to go to God in prayer for three days, and I promised to support them.

The husband decided to apply for a loan and he called me from the bank where he was about to apply. I advised him to return home and not sign anything since the instruction to move forward hadn't come yet. I could tell he was very upset. When they eventually found the house, I instructed them to make an offer, despite not having the down payment. They also reminded me of this fact, but I insisted they make an offer anyway. He made an offer, and the sellers accepted it. The sellers then requested that they pay $1000 to hold the house, and I advised him to put down that amount. God kept holding the house for them until they were able to make the full down payment. They eventually moved into the home to the glory of God.

In some cases, people give a specific amount as a seed or offering and expect to be placed on a pedestal. At CCCG, we don't do that. God watches over those things, elevating people accordingly. This is why the job of a Pastor can be challenging at times. I cringe when I hear people share their testimonies in a way that takes the glory for themselves instead of giving it to God. I share certain aspects of testimonies to ensure that everyone listening has the ability to replicate those testimonies. I let people know the keys that were used and the principles that were followed to achieve their results. When you examine the measures they implemented to achieve these outcomes, that's something noteworthy. The kingdom of God is impartial; you'll get the result if you take the steps. My job is to communicate to everyone, as much as possible, with the help of the Holy Ghost so that there is no favouritism.

HUMILITY VS PRIDE

Many people do not choose the path of humility because they do not understand its benefits. We have been taught to value pride over humility. People often say, "Nobody can ever take me for a ride," or "I could never let people treat me like that." We respond this way based on culture, upbringing, and other factors. However, Jesus showed us the importance of humility by saying that if someone slaps us, we should turn the other cheek in certain situations. Jesus did not specify the circumstances in which we should do so, but we know that God is not against fighting back when necessary. Sometimes, the Holy Ghost will instruct us to remain quiet, even if we are right. He may even ask us to apologize to someone who has wronged us. This is because God is teaching us a lesson in greatness.

Consider Joseph, for example. When he became Prime Minister, the Bible never mentioned that he sought revenge on his brothers, even though they had mistreated him. In fact, when their father was dying, his brothers were afraid that Joseph would seek retribution, but he assured them that God had allowed him to go through his experiences to prepare the way for them. Joseph demonstrated humility, accepting God's training to become great. Similarly, the pain we have experienced may be preparing us for greatness, but we must humble ourselves and accept God's training.

Walking in humility yields greater rewards than walking in pride. We should strive to cultivate humility, which involves being open to correction, not holding grudges, and being willing to learn. Humility allows us to accept God's training, which prepares us for greatness. Many people will intentionally hinder you from receiving what you need because they see pride, but when there is humility, people will offer you way more than they were planning to because that is how God had ordained it to be.

God gives grace to the humble, but He resists the proud. When I was a Youth Pastor, someone called me by my first name instead of addressing me as Pastor Emmanuel, as the Head Pastor had stated. I ignored her and felt justified, but the Holy Spirit reminded me that she had only called me by my name. I apologized to her for not responding, and she never again addressed me by my name. Now I know that if anyone calls me Emmanuel, Pastor, Reverend, or anything else, I won't care. In that case, however, I was offended because of pride.

HUMILITY:
CHILDLIKE CHARACTERISTICS

Trusting

They are very trusting. A child has no choice but to trust. What other option does a baby have when hungry besides breast milk? Can they find food somewhere else? The baby knows that they don't have any other option. That is what humility is. I know a particular Pastor who oversees a large Ministry in 192 nations. He is known to be a very humble man, and one day stated that he had no choice but to be humble.

Dependent

One sign of humility is that you can depend on others. Children are dependent. A child has no issue depending on others. Proud people want to stand alone. They will say that they don't want to be a burden to people. That is a revised way of saying they're proud and don't want anyone to be associated with their success.

Honesty

Another sign of humility is honesty. If you want to find out something about another person or situation, go to the kids. My parents are Pastors, so they trained us to tell inquisitive members or leaders that they should ask our parents when they asked probing questions. Some people are skilled interrogators. That being said children are beautifully honest. They tell the truth. And that's a sign of humility. Jesus taught about two people who went to pray; one went and told God how good he was, but another one confessed and said he was a sinner. Jesus asked which of those two people was honest; it was the one who came with humility. He came knowing that he wasn't perfect and that he needed help.

HUMILITY:
THE PROPHETIC GIFT

One of the most difficult aspects of a Pastor's job, especially for those with prophetic gifts, is correcting things in people's lives. This is why God gives grace to take certain approaches. God, for example, can show me something about someone, but I've learned not to go and challenge the person, especially when I am still engaged with the prophetic gift. This is because many of them will blatantly deny it, only to find out much later that it was one hundred percent true, but by then, your faith in the prophetic gift may have already taken a hit. Therefore, I ask questions and advise in line with what I know I've heard from God, which allows people to save face. It doesn't always have to be confrontational; there are examples in scripture to further explain this.

When Nathan, the prophet, confronted David about killing a man and taking his cattle, David didn't argue or put up a front. Instead, he surrendered, showing humility. When you compare humility to perfection in the kingdom of God, humility carries more weight. I say this because I have seen it in action. For instance, when Ahab allowed

Jezebel to kill a prophet and take his vineyard, God sent a prophet to tell Ahab what He was going to do as punishment. Ahab was a brutal king, yet he humbled himself when he heard the prophecy, tore his clothes, and put ash on himself. Even God recognized Ahab's humility and didn't punish him in his lifetime.

Humility is powerful; it makes God more vulnerable to us. Let's look at 1 Kings 21:17-29. What kind of God is this? The Bible is awesome in telling us how powerful humility is. Even though Ahab didn't change his wicked ways, he humbled himself. God would have moved the curse from generation to generation if his son had also humbled himself. When it comes to leadership, we have to talk about humility because the more you humble yourself, the higher God will take you. The higher He takes you, the more humility He will request from you. It's the same as when God blesses you financially; He will require you to give more. So when God wants to lift you higher and exalt you, He will request more humility from you.

BENEFITS OF HUMILITY

There is no limit to how high God can take a person. A few years ago, God told me that if I kept walking with Him, I would become like the moon, reflecting His light, just like the moon reflects the light of the sun. He also said that if I keep walking with Him, He would allow me to become the sun, thereby reflecting my own light. Elijah reached that level, which is why Elisha was able to ask, "*...Where is the Lord God of Elijah?*" (2 Kings 2:14) In Philippians 2, it is said that Jesus humbled himself and was given a name that is above every other name. At the mention of the name of Jesus, every knee shall bow, and every tongue shall confess. That is what humility looks like in the kingdom of God. The more we humble ourselves, the higher God takes us. He can begin to use our image to deliver people, even in their dreams, and it has nothing to do with us.

I was humbled when a couple came to church, and the wife said that she saw me and the name of the church in a dream. She went online to search for the name of the church, and when she found it, she came with her husband. Thank God for spiritual wives; someone telling me they saw me in a dream, laying hands on them, and casting out demons, and I didn't even know they had demons! This is the beautiful side that comes as a result of humility.

After a particular service, three people disrespected me, but I had no offence. I correct people, but the Holy Spirit tells me to swallow it and not respond in certain settings, so I move on. Isaiah 53 is a passage that tells me that God wants me to grow more in humility. All He is looking for is if He can trust a person with power or if they will be like Elisha, who got angry and cursed all the children in front of him. He is asking if He can really trust us with power. At one Bible study, someone went through a spiritual attack. The Holy Spirit later revealed to me that the person was attacked because they disrespected me. If I were aware of it, I would have corrected the person to prevent them from experiencing that attack.

The beautiful side is the glory that comes from it. But we must understand when God is taking us through those steps to humility because the enemy will make us believe that people are taking advantage of us. He is a liar, so he doesn't show us the glory that comes if God's hand is in it too. God looks for humility in people, and one of the dangerous things I see in leadership is that you can easily become a god to people. That is very dangerous. God himself can allow this to happen like He told Moses that the Israelites were Moses' people. God also made Moses like a god to Pharaoh. That's the dangerous thing about leadership, especially when you begin to get results. God will glorify you so much that people can begin to see you as a god because of the solutions you bring to them. But if you keep humbling yourself, you'll be able to avoid certain roadblocks and land mines that some people go through in their acceleration in life.

Jesus increased in wisdom, stature, and favour with God and man because He was subject to His parents. Even when He was not wrong, He did not act arrogantly or refuse to be accountable to His parents. He asked questions in the temple but still went back to them. Being under authority is a quick way to cultivate humility, and we can learn from Jesus' example.

God gave me insight into the benefits of staying humble, and it keeps me in check, especially when I make a mistake that has to do with the church. I've made a vow that I will share it with the whole church. Those are some of the things that pride does not like. Pride wants to cover up its mistakes so that they can see you as a perfect person. So I share those things when God corrects me.

When I was writing the book "A Disciplined Life" and shared those things, my wife read it and asked why I included that God told me I was not disciplined enough. It was the truth. At some point in my life, God looked at me and said I was not disciplined enough for where He wanted to take me. It's good that people know that because it's relevant to the book, so they should not lose heart if they find themselves in that same situation. For me, that's one of the revelations I've received. Because pride does not like those things. Pride wants to be praised. It does not like people to know that there are areas of weakness. The truth is, darkness never leaves, we just have to keep the light on. Whenever pride tries to bring out its ugly head, make sure that you take the steps God tells you to so that it never gets ahold of you.

PRIDE & SELF-PITY

Now why is self-pity pride? Self-pity comes from someone looking down on themselves. Someone with low self-esteem believes that they should be somewhere or a certain way but cannot see themselves in that light. Therefore, they put themselves down in response to that. Self-pity is an outcome of certain conditions or a way of thinking that undermines someone's worth. It is pride because the person believes they should have been something they are currently not. So they do to themselves what others do to them when they look down on them.

A proud person is doing the same thing as someone with self-pity but in the opposite direction. A proud person says, "This is who I am, and everyone else must acknowledge it." A person with self-pity says, "This is who I am, but no one acknowledges it, so I will just do it myself." This is similar to comedians who start by saying negative things about themselves to avoid being judged by others. It is self-deprecating behaviour, and that is why it is pride. When the condition changes, the real reason why it is pride is revealed, and the person may begin to behave differently. It is worth noting that poor people can be proud. People whose financial needs are not met can be the proudest, but their pride may not be visible until their financial situation changes. For example, a man in Zimbabwe once sewed an outfit made of money. This behaviour is not limited to any particular country, there are all kinds of people everywhere.

I want to communicate the steps to achieve mind-blowing results. Humility is one of them. We've discussed spiritual warfare, and temptations usually signal the start of spiritual warfare, and part of the bait is a temptation to pride. Sometimes the devil will present that to a person. As one of our members said, not all communications are the same. Some phrases are laced with pride; the spirit behind them is pride, intending to elevate your heart if you're not careful. Often, people will reach out and tell me that it was a great message and that they were blessed by what I said. However, when some praise me, and I know that it is not coming from a good source, I shut it down.

THE SPIRIT OF PRIDE

Let's talk about another dimension of pride. There is a demonic government called the spirit of pride. Many people find it difficult to be humble because they are being oppressed by this spirit. Not every compliment from believers comes from a humble spirit. There are times when the spirit of pride is involved. How can you tell if the spirit of pride is involved? Intensity and frequency. There is a difference between someone being occasionally proud but some people are always proud, and you can see it in how they talk, eat, and walk. They embody pride!

The number 12 holds significance. Jesus had 12 disciples, and Jacob had 12 sons who eventually formed the tribe of Israel. The number is synonymous with the government of the kingdom of God. In the demonic realm, the government comprises 12 key spirits present in every dimension and area. There are minions and smaller spirits, as well as chief ones. One of them is the spirit of sexual immorality, which is a government on its own. Another one is the spirit of fear, a chief spirit, and the spirit of pride is also among them. This indicates that there is no kingdom or country where you won't find one of those 12 spirits attempting to dominate that place. They are the rulers in the kingdom of darkness. Esau also had 12 chiefs, indicating that pride resides high up.

Pride can bring down dominions, regardless of how high or exalted they are. How do we know? Because those are the spirits sent whenever a person is destined to reign. King Nebuchadnezzar, for example, was brought down by the spirit of pride. In Acts 11, Herod was also brought down by the spirit of pride. Sexual immorality, fear, and pride are all spirits. Sometimes, no matter how many messages a person hears, the spirit of pride is what is plaguing them. If you are reading this chapter and are getting very angry, it means that the spirit of pride is holding you captive. This is one of the ways to know that you are dealing with a spirit.

Identifying the Spirit of Pride

As you read this information, you may also become uncomfortable as you keep reading. This discomfort is evidence of a spirit of pride at work. Those who are not uncomfortable hearing these words simply need to learn, assimilate, and pick up points so they can keep building up humility. That's the main difference. So, if you feel uncomfortable, you are either oppressed or possessed by the spirit of pride. All you need to do is rebuke it under your breath, saying, "You foul spirit of pride, you can never control me anymore. I take authority over you in the mighty name of Jesus. Amen!"

Remember that what you're reading is meant to help you. You don't want the spirit of pride; you want humility. When you are delivered, you will begin to receive what I am saying. The Bible says, *"Pride goes before destruction, And a haughty spirit before a fall."* (Proverbs 16:18). When you are proud, you are telling God you have reached the apex of where you can ever get to. If that's what you're telling God, He will agree that that's the highest you will ever attain. Soon, that person will begin to decline. That will not be our portion in Jesus' name. Amen!

Dealing With the Spirit of Pride

According to Philippians 2:1-3, one of the revelations needed to operate in humility is to know that there is someone greater than us at every point in time. There is always someone greater than us. Let the understanding settle in your spirit that there is someone greater than you. God is greater than all. I am not saying someone is better than you. That's different. There's someone 'greater' than you. When you have that understanding, you will know that while you may be very good in a specific area, there are some areas where someone else is better.

So, for instance, you may be extremely good at mixing audio, but someone else knows how to fix routers and do IT networking, and you have no idea about those things. You may be extremely knowledgeable in psychology and its concepts and principles, but somebody else knows how to send rockets to space, and you know nothing about that. You may be an expert in working with children, while someone else is great in another area. One of the things that pride does is make a person feel like they're better than everyone at everything.

One of the things I have become accustomed to doing is understanding the areas in which those around me are excelling so that I can honour them in those areas. This helps me to assess myself properly and maintain balance. For example, I once heard a woman singing in her house while her mother was on the phone. When a friend asked the mother what song was playing on the radio, she told them it was her daughter singing. I know I cannot sing like that yet! If I were to start singing, you'd probably want me to stop and turn down the volume.

I am aware of my area of expertise. If I am called upon in the middle of the night to preach, for example, I can respond without any preparation needed. I am not skilled in cooking or baking like some of the people in our Ministry, who can create a cake so good that it can be eaten within a day. I am aware of my strengths and the areas in which others excel beyond me, and this keeps me balanced. It also prevents anyone from deceiving me by telling me that I am better at baking cakes than a professional baker. Such deception is not a declaration of faith but a lie. I know who I am, but I'm also aware of who other people are.

My question for you is, do you know the capacities and capabilities of other people without bringing yourself down? These are the things that I study and observe when I look at people, including children. It is a fantastic habit that has helped me identify the giftings of others. This is what Philippians 2:3 says, *"In lowliness of mind let each esteem others better than himself."* I have a bachelor's degree in accounting but never think I am better than a chartered accountant. Therefore, I do not perform the role of an accountant at CCCG. I also have an IT degree, but I would never think I am better than someone trained in IT. I know my place. When it comes to my area of expertise, I confidently stand in front and function in my own capacity. When it is somebody else's area, I take a step back and *"let each esteem others better than himself."* (Philippians 2:3)

Do a quick exercise; look around you and observe others. What do you think other people can do better than you? Try to come up with a few examples quickly. Do you know how the enemy deceives people? He tells you that it's pride if you feel like you're better than others in specific areas, but he doesn't tell you the other side of the coin. Therefore, pause for a second, look around you, and acknowledge the strengths of others. This is one way to remain balanced. It's good to recognize that some people are better than you in certain areas.

God is better than every one of us in everything! When the enemy says that you're not good in a specific area that someone else is, you can confirm and say, "Yes, that person is better than me in that area." This way, you don't feel self-pity. You know that person is better than you in that area because you know what area you are better than that person in. Some of us feel guilty when we acknowledge certain things about ourselves or how good we are at certain things. Jesus said that He is the bread of life and that He is the way, the truth, and the life. That is Jesus, and He said that we should be like Him. He is our boss. Say this out loud, "I am good, and others are also very good."

SEVEN DEADLY MOTIVES OF LEADERSHIP

Power

You must never aspire to be a leader because you want power over people. Leadership must never be the solution to get back at people who look down on you. Some people are power-hungry, like Jezebel.

Prestige

What does prestige mean? It refers to the exaltation that comes from being in a particular position. In the CCCG auditorium, there are two chairs where my wife and I sit. These chairs are different from those of the congregants. It was not my idea, but someone from the church offered to buy them from us saying it was an instruction from God. Some leaders would glory in that situation because they desire special treatment because of their position. Some others, however, do not want to sit there because it exposes them as being in a higher position than others. Only the one wearing the shoe knows where it hurts. For instance, a woman wearing high heels may look great, but she may later have to ask her husband to massage her feet when she takes them off. Being a spiritual father, for example, is a significant responsibility. When everyone else is sleeping, God may wake you up and instruct you to pray for a particular person. Prestige is the beauty that comes from a position, but it's often a trap set by the devil to distract people from their true purpose.

Position

This is when an individual wants to have a title or be the head of an organization, Ministry, or a particular country.

Popularity

Wanting people to know your name and who you are. In school, I was not popular and thought that everybody would know who I was if I got into a specific position. That must never be the motive for leadership.

Pride

We spoke about pride previously. The Bible has much to say about pride; in one place, it says God resists the proud, and in another place, pride comes before the fall. In this case, the person's confidence is in their position, not in God, who gave them the position.

Personal Gain

Leadership should never be for personal gain; a true leader is a servant leader. One day, the Lord said to me that he called me to be a platform for others to rise. So my job is that people stand on me to get to the top. I told the leaders to take advantage of me. That is my job! All those people the devil has convinced are disturbing me and don't understand that it is my job. The platform is there, so people can see you when you stand on it. A leader is a platform for others to stand on. Someone said they could see further because they were standing on the shoulders of giants. My parents prayed for me and my siblings that we would get to heights that they never reached because they were platforms for us. Some of the things we are doing today by God's grace, are because of them, and many of these things are things they never experienced. Ordinarily, by the grace of God, when I get to their age or higher, I will win more souls than they were able to win for God.

The career of the called is greater in the latter than the former. For those coming behind me, my job, if they desire, is to show them how to reach the things I attained way sooner than I did. Being a leader is being like a pipe. The pipe's job is to let the water flow, not to hold the water. Your own benefit is that you will get wet every now and then. When you help someone in their journey to get their degrees through mentoring, prayers, and other forms of assistance, it is that person's name on the certificate at the end of the day. Our job as leaders is not for personal gain. Anything that comes back to you is because God decided for that person to sow a seed back into you. The Bible says freely you have received, freely give.

Paycheck

Money must not be the motive for leadership. The love of money is very dangerous and is one of the reasons why people give false prophecies and manipulate people.

Real humility cannot exist outside of being under authority. It goes hand in hand with everything else we will discuss later. Being humble is not the same as being naive. Those who were colonized were subdued forcefully. Therefore, we cannot say they were humble because they did not willingly give up anything, it was taken from them. Someone coming to subdue you forcefully is not the same as acting in humility. Allowing this to happen is actually being naive and taken advantage of. That's why the Bible talks about humbling ourselves. We are the ones who give it up ourselves. We choose to be humble and under authority. Only the devil uses force and manipulation to take away a person's autonomy.

We have to know the difference between willingly being humble and giving up certain rights and privileges. Jesus said that nobody takes His life from Him, but He gave it up willingly. The moment it becomes forceful, it means there is another agenda happening. Witchcraft is akin to manipulation, which is tied to control. In Acts 6, the lady with the spirit of divination followed Paul for multiple days. Only demons behave that way, forcefully. Even when they said no, they still continued. For instance, a person should not try to manipulate you by saying,

"You should do this because it is the humble thing to do." That is not true humility. It should be your personal decision, not something to be manipulated.

The way up in the kingdom of God is down in humility; you take yourself down so you can be lifted up. In Philippians 2:5-7, Jesus made Himself of no reputation, even though He was equal to God. That is why people with low self-esteem cannot claim to be humble because it was not their choice. They couldn't even do it if they wanted to. The destination of humility is death to self and the concerns of this life. The way up is down; therefore, death to self is the ultimate destination of the humble. However, if I tell you this is easy, I will be lying to you. God is taking you to the point of death to self.

Many people today must not be able to heal anyone of headaches. Why? Because the moment that happens, they will start their own religion, and everything will be about them. There is a particular story of a Pastor whose bodyguards beat up people on the streets whenever he showed up. The people couldn't even look at his vehicle. When he got into the church building, people would lie down on the floor, and he would step on them to get to the pulpit because he was 'so anointed' that his feet could not touch the ground. One day he burned a woman while trying to cast out a demon from her. He was arrested and sentenced to death, not by humility, but by hanging. It's good to understand the theory from a practical perspective.

THE WAYS TO HUMILITY

Fasting

Fasting is a quick way to humility because when you fast, you are denying your flesh. Someone who is fasting is physically weak and cannot respond to every argument that is going on. You just want to eat! Prideful people always want revenge and always have something to say. They might not say it for others to hear, but on the inside, they always respond to everything. One of the ways pride manifests is when someone corrects them, they begin to look at the person's own mistakes. It just happens automatically. In their mind, they're wondering how you could dare correct them. That is pride; humility is the opposite. God breaks our pride the longer we fast and the more frequently we fast.

Being Under Authority

We spoke in more detail about being under spiritual authority in a previous lesson. Being under authority involves correction. When nobody is there to correct you, you are at risk of the destruction that comes from pride. The more you are corrected, and accept correction, the closer you will get to that path of humility.

If you are not under the authority of a human being, not just God, you will never be humble because the flesh will never allow you to do that. Your work has to be able to be reviewed by others. There are different levels of humility. Some people get to the point where they can submit to a specific person because they like them or see them as a wise leader, but they cannot submit to their own colleagues. That is still pride. What happens when God puts a leader that you don't think you like, or is not qualified or as gifted as you are? Will you still submit? Even Jesus manifested disobedience, but He didn't continue that way. He put it aside and was subject to them. They went to Nazareth every year, meaning that He didn't stay back in Jerusalem the next year. He went back with everybody else. Humility is good. Your flesh will not like it. It will be uncomfortable and get you angry, but just remain humble.

Working With Others on the Team

During interviews, people are often asked if they prefer working alone or as part of a team. Group work can take place in school or at work, and it requires considering other people's opinions, even when you feel more knowledgeable than they are. Some students in my lectures express a desire to leave their groups, and while some provide reasons, others simply do not wish to collaborate with others. Learning to work with others requires humility, and straying from this can lead to behaviours that contradict biblical teachings on humility.

Luke 2:41-52 recounts an instance in which Jesus, our Saviour, was corrected by his parents for remaining in Jerusalem without permission. Nowhere does it mention that He apologized. Jesus was human, subject to the same bodily functions and desires as everyone else. His argumentative response to his parents' reprimand is relatable and comforting, showing us that even Jesus struggled with humility. However, it is never too late to start practicing humility, and Jesus is an excellent example to follow. At this point in His life, Jesus was a normal human being who had not yet received the baptism of the Holy Spirit. After the incident in Jerusalem, He returned to Nazareth with His parents and was subject to them. He never behaved in the same manner again. In John 2, when Jesus' mother asked Him to turn water into wine, He responded that His time had not yet come. This shows that Jesus remained accountable to His mother, even after He had become the Messiah.

4

Servant Leadership

It's almost as if these two words should not be placed side-by-side. Many people think being a leader means that everyone should serve them. A leader is meant to be the chief servant. We lead because we've seen a need that needs to be fulfilled, and we want to take the lead in fulfilling that need. The leaders I see are those who make sure that the focus of their leadership always remains on the need to be fulfilled.

For instance, a mother leads in her home and leads her children, and a father leads the family. We're there to serve, not necessarily to be served. The moment what you're receiving is way more than what you're giving; you're already on the way out as a leader. This is a very dangerous equation. The Bible says it is more blessed to give than to receive. The moment you receive more than you are giving, you're no longer being balanced as a leader, and most likely, the person's replacement is already being trained. This is the way God works.

Who is a servant? A servant is one whose focus is on making those they are serving satisfied. This is a word that many people do not like to hear. The focus is very prideful in this society. Many people are raised to focus on themselves and what's in it for them. That's not the way to leadership. A leadership role is a servant role - What is in it for those I lead? How can I be a blessing to someone else? How else can I serve them? Servant leadership is about leading with humility, hence the word servant. Jesus was the one who brought this principle forward when He taught His disciples to serve others instead of arguing about who was the greatest in Mark 9:33-35.

EFFECTIVE LEADERSHIP THROUGH DELEGATION

One of the ways we demonstrate servant leadership is by delegation. This is strange because some people believe that they should do everything by themselves and kill themselves while doing the work. That does not make sense if you truly love the people you're serving. According to the Word of God, servant leadership is not about doing everything yourself. It is about spreading the responsibility for the work to ensure it gets done. The truth is, if you want to do everything, then the people will obviously not be served properly. You will be tired and burnt out, but you're still there trying to serve people.

In Exodus 18, the Bible tells us about Moses' journey into servant leadership. The journey first started with God calling him, then going to Egypt and letting the people go, but he almost destroyed the same people he was leading because he wanted to do everything by himself. If there's something that you would notice about the life of Moses, it is his leadership journey. He was always in a state of frustration. Why? Because he was carrying the burdens alone. But in Exodus 18, his father-in-law observed how he led the people, serving and judging them by himself from morning to night. The father looked at him and said that if he continued in this way, he would be frustrated, unable to lead the people, and die young. Jethro, his father-in-law, suggested that he delegate responsibility to trained leaders. Moses decided to follow that suggestion.

Servant leaders are not self-centred but love to share the load and the burden of leadership. Somebody trained you, and you made some mistakes before you became effective. We also have to train and raise other people and give them room to make mistakes. This way, they will become all God has called them to be.

One of the reasons why I love servant leadership is that there can be no success in leadership without a successor. Servant leadership helps us lead while raising those who will take over after us. Our focus is on the health and success of the organization or group of people we lead. If we're not there, what will happen? A servant leader plans for that eventuality. If we go on vacation, will things still function correctly? In Acts 6:1-7, we see the same situation. The work increased because the disciples stepped away from what they weren't supposed to be doing, and many more people became saved. That's why servant leadership includes delegating responsibility. There must be diversity in gender, race, experience, background, grace, and anointing for exponential growth in productivity. That can only happen through delegation.

Before we get too far, let's talk about delegation. Before delegating, we need to know how to select the people. In Exodus 18:20, Jethro told Moses the characteristics of the people he should delegate to:

HOW TO SELECT LEADERS

- **People Who Fear God:** You should select people who don't just go to church but also fear God.
- **People of Truth:** Some people can lie so well that you can't even imagine! Even when you catch them in a lie, they are very slippery. You must choose people of truth and integrity.
- **People Who Hate Covetousness:** This one is crucial! I only realized it many years ago. When we lead people and succeed, the glory of God shows up in our lives. It's essential that those leading alongside us hate covetousness. Otherwise, they will begin to become like Judas. The main thing that got Judas angry was that Jesus was favoured and honoured so much, and he

wasn't honoured that way. If we haven't experienced this, we may not understand what I'm talking about unless God gives us understanding.

Let us go more in-depth into covetousness because it is an important point.

COVETOUSNESS

Covetousness is wanting something that belongs to someone else and wanting it really bad. Like someone else's girlfriend, boyfriend, car, or house. Exactly what that person wants, they want to have. We must ensure that we are around people who can be comfortable when we are blessed. Otherwise, we are digging our graves. They're around when people come to bless us; they see all those things and just stand there and wish it was them. However, when we were working hard before the blessings came, they wouldn't say, "If only that was them!" Until our feet are in someone else's issues, we don't know what it feels like. It always looks easy.

Someone once had a dream. They saw me preaching, and it looked awesome; I was well-dressed. They began to see arrows coming from the congregation being fired at me. Of course, the arrows didn't touch me. The person woke up and realized that the work of being a Pastor is way deeper than what we see. Of course, sometimes, the devil pushes people into covetousness. We must get people who hate covetousness and have been tested for such things. God will give us strategies on how to test the people. No one can say they are not a thief until they have had the opportunity to steal and choose not to.

When I was a Youth Pastor at a different ministry, one of the youths' mothers would come and give food to the main Pastor. Despite being their Youth Pastor and taking care of them, I watched her give the food to someone else. I heard the devil say that I was doing all the work, but somebody else was reaping all the benefits. I would respond by saying, "No, you're a liar! That's my Pastor, and he deserves everything he receives." It wasn't easy, but I was being tested and didn't even know it.

There's another aspect of covetousness where people come to me and want to tell me something, but they don't want me to tell the main Pastor. I would respond by saying, "If you can't tell the Pastor, then don't tell me. If you tell me, he must hear it if he needs to hear it." That is another aspect of covetousness where they covet people's hearts. It can never be from God because you're trying to pit people against each other.

Absalom, one of the sons of David, did this when people would come to meet the king, but he would take them aside, claiming that the king didn't have time and solve the problems himself. Therefore, you need to check around you and make sure those people are individuals who hate covetousness, which means they can be trusted. You don't want to experience the consequences before you learn you're not to have covetous leaders on your team. What are some practical ways that you can test this? First, pay attention to how people respond when you are appreciated, or accolades are coming to you. Look around and observe how people respond when those things are happening. There's a lot we can see and learn when we pay attention.

Second, look at the way information is managed. There are different types of covetousness. Some covet what you have, some covet you and everything that makes you, you. If someone hears something negative about you as a friend and does not think it necessary to mention it to you, that is a dangerous sign of covetousness. The challenge many times is we don't recognize these seeds, we only recognize trees when they are fully mature. The thing is that seed, once it is planted, will grow to become a tree, and uprooting a tree is way more work. Once you know the seed, you can stop it from being planted or even take it away. Information management is key. If you hear something that could benefit someone, do you communicate it to them?

If you have identified covetous traits within people who are already around you, you don't necessarily need to cut them off. It depends on how close they are to you. Some people can still be around but not too close to you because the closer they are, the more danger they can pose. Or maybe they have a skill set or gift that you need, so you can still seek to work with them, but they cannot be a central contributor because that's where the danger lies.

Signs of Covetousness

How do you check for these things in yourself? The heart of man is desperately evil. When you realize that you are displaying the same traits that were mentioned, that is a sign of covetousness. When someone is being praised, how do you feel on the inside? If you can identify covetousness in yourself, then you can rebuke the devil. I will celebrate with people who are celebrating and rejoice with people who are rejoicing! When they are lifted, it does not affect you being lifted.

We are all human and not perfect. We are walking towards perfection. The Bible says we should be perfect as our heavenly Father is perfect. It's a journey. Any thoughts that are negative and condemning can never be from God. Permitted conviction will come and encourage you to be better, but condemnation is like judgment. It doesn't give you the room to say that you want to improve. It wants to judge you. Know that it's condemnation you need to deal with.

Another sign of covetousness is hoarding information and choosing not to share it with others. You should ask yourself why you don't want to share information with someone. One day, a few years ago, ahead of a visitation, the Lord shared some revelations with me. He said, "Do you know one of the reasons why I share these things with you? It's because I am confident that you will share these things with other people and won't hold it to yourself."

Some people will copy you no matter what you do. Because God designed us to lead people, regardless of their actions, people will be drawn to your every move. We need to be able to separate that from the dishonest version of someone copying you to overshadow and remove you from the picture. Otherwise, it is safe because you are doing your job and leading people into their own destinies. When you see people copying you out of a genuine place, begin to show them their own uniqueness instead of telling them that they are copying you because that could damage their self-image. Identify the things that are unique in them and encourage them to pursue the path of uniqueness. Those types of people lack confidence, which is why they do what they are doing. Even Paul said, "Be ye followers of me, as I follow Christ."

In the context of mentorship, I advise people to copy my principles, not my personality, because those are two different things. Nobody has a monopoly on principles because we all got them from scriptures. There is no plagiarism when it comes to the Bible. If I am an introvert and you are an extrovert, you don't need to copy everything I am doing and stay quiet. Copy principles, but don't copy personalities. You need to be original and comfortable in your own skin. When my wife began to minister, she was very animated and dramatic. She came to me discouraged and upset that she couldn't just be quiet and still. I told her to be herself; now she's comfortable and can express herself energetically. A servant leader cares more about the good of the organization and its people than their own enrichment.

How to Curb Covetousness

One of the things we have to do in servant leadership to curb covetousness is to bring people into the work. They need to see the input as well, and it will help. I was humbled when someone who just joined the church was considering whether she would serve or not. She was almost changing her mind because she overheard some of the leaders talking about all the sacrifices and the work involved. I was very happy when she said that to me because people should know what they desire to get into. The leaders come on Sunday mornings, stay for several services, and stay back in the evening to pray and plan for the church and the land. The Bible says to consider those who labour among us in Word and in prayer to be given double honour. God knows the effort they're putting in, so they deserve the honour. If you dishonour your Pastors and elders, God Himself will dishonour you.

APPRECIATION & ENCOURAGEMENT

As we begin to lead and get results in leadership, people will come back to say thank you. People will try their best to make you as comfortable as possible, but it's not every comfort that should be accepted. Some people, without knowing, maybe pushing you out of your leadership through the comfort you're receiving. As we bless people, we must make sure that we still stay relevant in service to the people.

I use Elon Musk as an example quite a few times because I admire his achievements in the secular world. When they had issues with the Tesla production, he would sleep in the factory, even as a billionaire, ensuring the work was getting done. At that level, he was still working for 16 hours or more every single day. The moment the people you are leading begin to work harder than you, you are already walking on dangerous ground. When the people went to sleep, Jesus was still working, either in prayer or something else.

Servant leaders must ensure they go a few steps further than the people they are leading in sacrifice. I can't imagine anybody in this church giving more than we do. That cannot happen. It's not a curse, God called me first before everybody else, not just to give resources but also time, giftings, and many other things. When leadership is taught properly, it will help you see those who want to go into it with the wrong mindset because many people see the accolades and the special parking spot! For some people, that is all they are looking at, but they don't see the work that goes on behind the scenes. Our job is not to look for accolades but to serve. Whether people say thank you or not, we are here to serve. A servant leader should not need encouragement. This one is tough. A CEO's job is to tell everybody else, "Thank you." It can be a burden if we constantly seek appreciation from people. Instead, servant leaders should strive to reach a point where they don't need encouragement or appreciation from others to continue serving.

This is illustrated in an online post about a black American who pointed out that they care for their mothers and children without receiving any appreciation. Someone responded by saying that taking care of their family is what they are supposed to do and thanked them for doing their job. Similarly, many take care of their spouses without expecting any appreciation. It is important to remember that we should appreciate God for who He is and how He deals with people every day. We should strive to have a mindset of gratitude and appreciation towards God and others without expecting anything in return.

If you find yourself needing encouragement, where would be a healthy place to receive it? There is a way that we can grow to a point where we don't actually need encouragement. However, if we still need it sometimes, it's fine. When I was much younger, I used to eat a lot. Then I would watch some older folks, like my father, who would just have one slice of bread for breakfast. But now I find myself able to go for some time without food, and people have to ask me if I've eaten. I never imagined that I could get to this point. There are days when I go much longer before realizing that I haven't eaten. In the same way, we can grow to a point where we don't need encouragement to function. Seek approval and guidance from approved and ordained sources, not from people who want to manipulate you.

SELF-SERVING VS SERVANT LEADERSHIP

Let's look at a few differences between servant leadership and self-serving leadership. For a self-serving leader, it's all about 'me,' but for a servant leader, it's about 'we.' A self-serving leader wants others to serve them, and you can hear it in their words or how they complain about a lack of appreciation. However, a servant leader is focused on serving others. A self-serving leader is only happy when they win. A servant leader is happy when the whole team scores, not just when 'they' score the goal themselves. A self-serving leader wants to ride on the shoulders of everybody else and take advantage of everyone, but a servant leader wants to carry people on their shoulders. A self-serving leader's needs always come first, but for a servant leader, the needs of others come first.

In some cultures, like in Nigeria, the father eats the most meat for dinner, lunch, or breakfast, and that's how you know who the head of the house is. Some people may talk about how Elijah asked the woman to cook for him first. However, Elijah was not coming to be served in this instance; he was coming to serve the woman, and she needed to sow into his life to become blessed. Self-serving leaders are there for their own career and ambition, but servant leader is there for the organization's or group's ambition. A self-serving leader micromanages people, but a servant leader empowers people.

PRINCIPLES:
TO HELP YOU SERVE OTHERS WELL

Accept Those You Serve

One of the main reasons why leaders find it hard to serve others is that the people haven't accepted them. Many leaders do not feel they have much in common with the people they are charged to lead because people are different. As a leader, I have found that this is one of the biggest impediments to effective leadership. Some people can only lead those from their own country, or a particular age group, or the same gender as them, and the list goes on. Some can only lead educated people, and the moment they encounter people who are not as educated, they just get frustrated. One of the things we have to keep in mind is that we're all different people.

For me, one way to know that someone is close to God is by the way they love and the way they accept people's differences because God is a God of diversity. It's funny that many people try to do and be the opposite. They want to do something that creates the same, but from the very beginning, God created diversity. We are all as different as the homes we were raised in. Many people need to be more compassionate and understand that if other people were raised the same way they were raised, the other people wouldn't have turned out the way they are. If they had a loving father and a present mother in their lives, maybe they would have been better than they are today. We are all different. There are some things I grew up seeing in my home that made it easier for me to be who I am today, things that some people never saw.

Imagine people whose parents are divorced deciding to come together in marriage. They had better go through marriage counselling; otherwise, the marriage will be very difficult because they don't have a template on the inside of them that they have seen work. We are all different. Our parents, the homes we are raised in, our economic situations growing up, and how our extended family functioned have defined who we all are today. Some people were sent to their grandparents, and that's how they feel so secure in the fact that they are loved. That is a specialty of grandparents: they make you feel loved and pampered. Some didn't have that privilege.

This also goes for your education level and even your church history. Some were raised in hyper-grace-filled churches, while some were raised in churches where everything was so strict that your hair could not be like this or like that; otherwise, you would go to hell. Some people were raised with the understanding of tithing from a young age, and they saw their parents giving tithes regularly, so it's common sense. Others grew up in an environment where the mother dared not touch the father's property. So, when they come to church, any talk about giving, they just squeeze their faces because they don't understand.

We need to understand these kinds of differences when we are leading people. That's why I love to hear people's stories. Suddenly, they will go from being animated to becoming real human beings in your own eyes. My question to you is: what makes you different as a person? What would a leader need to know to ensure that the person is handled with care?

A gentleman came to me because he felt like some members of the church did not represent the church properly. He was angry, showed me pictures, and told me to do something about that situation. I spoke with my spiritual father on that topic, and he told me that man is a person that I should avoid. That man is no longer in the church today. He had multiple sexual partners while accusing others of not effectively representing the church. When the man brought up the issue of certain individuals who were allegedly not representing the church well, I expressed my gratitude to him for informing me. However, it is worth noting that those same individuals are now strong in their faith, while the man who brought up the issue is no longer practicing his faith. I took the opportunity to educate him on our approach to such situations, emphasizing that our goal is not to destroy people but to lead them in a kind and constructive manner so they can continue growing. Unfortunately, he was not interested in this approach and instead advocated for a harsher, more punitive response.

People's backgrounds play a huge role in how they act, not just in the flesh but also in the spirit. It's important to know the people you're dealing with so you can properly serve them. For example, some church members don't want to hear from their Pastor regularly because they associate the Pastor's calls with trouble, while others feel offended if they're not contacted frequently. We need to meet people at their level and give them what they want, not what we think they want.

Allow People to Shine

In Exodus 18, the first criterion that Jethro advised Moses to use was to pick able men who were actually capable of doing the job. This includes allowing them to make mistakes, just like we all do. It's important to allow people to shine, which ties in with humility because when the people under you are shining, it helps you remain humble. Let's take the example of Saul, who encountered a situation where someone under him, David faced Goliath and killed him while Saul himself was running away. What Saul did not bargain for was what was going to come next.

Saul allowed David to go and fight the battle, and he supported him. After David killed Goliath, the women began to sing, *"Saul has slain his thousands, And David his ten thousands."* (1 Samuel 18:7) Saul was not pleased and thought, "The next thing, he wants to take the Kingdom from me!" Was Saul justified in the way he felt? Yes. How about David? What did David do wrong in that scenario? They say that silence means consent. David accepted what they were saying, so he deserved what he got. I am not endorsing what Saul did, but David acted foolishly. He should have gone to tell those women to stop singing since Saul was the king. Saul refused to understand that if someone under him killed the giant, then he, too, was a giant killer, as David was under his authority.

What could Saul have done? If I were Saul, I would have stopped the women from singing out of my love for David. Because he was already a king, he shouldn't accept those types of things in his heart. He should have done that, but he had an inferiority complex. Even though he was being crowned as king, he was hiding.

Some leaders will take credit for everything that is done. The best way to prevent this from overtaking you is to stay focused, stay in your lane, and compete with yourself. The moment our actions are tailored toward how a person will perceive something, we're already going in the wrong direction. No matter how good your intentions are, not everything you do will be understood by people. Especially as a leader, some people will not accept what you're doing, but you know what you're doing is right. For example, in this instance, Saul could have corrected the women, and they might have thought he was jealous of David, but later down the line, they would understand what he did. People don't like being corrected, so as long as it's right, keep doing it regardless of what you do.

One day, I took my dad's brand-new Honda Accord. They only drove those cars on Sundays, and they would cover it with a tarp during the week. That's what I used to learn how to drive. I would remove the cover, take it out for a spin, and later put it back. I continued to do it until one fateful day, I took the car for a wash. Moments later, my dad stepped out, looked around, and saw his car missing. I didn't know this had happened, so I came back and parked the car at 1:00 P.M., and went about my day. I got to the house, and he was waiting for me upstairs. He asked me how my day was, and I said it was great. Then he asked me if I drove the car, and I denied it. After I realized he was aware, I recalibrated. Thinking back now, I know I could have had an accident, but his response was merciful.

Sometimes, the people we are leading will not understand the steps we are taking. There is an artist named Nathaniel Bassey whose Pastor restricted him from ministering for many years, telling him that God was saying he was not yet ready. The Pastor would bring international artists to minister, but Nathaniel Bassey was never allowed to minister. Nathaniel Bassey shared the story many years later and talked about how he was angry and thought that the Pastor was afraid that if Nathaniel had accepted invitations, he would never reappear at the church. Despite the pain, he still decided to follow the instructions.

After a few years, the Pastor travelled to the United States, bought a trumpet, and told him that the Lord said he should give it to Nathaniel as a seed, as he was now ready to minister. I have not heard any of his songs that don't take me to the presence of God. Some people sing only one song, and that's all you know them for, but with Nathaniel Bassey, album after album, you can see God moving through him in every song. I do what God says I should do because my job is to make sure that I do what is required to preserve people's destinies. It's up to you if you want to make your own decisions.

The enemy was putting so much pressure on someone about why they weren't allowed to preach. The person was open enough to tell me that they were struggling because I kept asking other people to minister and not them. I sat the person down and let them know that a time was coming when they would be ministering every single day. I told them that they should relax because the time had not yet come and that when the time came, they would preach until they were tired of preaching - leadership classes, counselling sessions, Bible studies, morning service, second service, third service, and so on.

Servant leadership is leading with humility. I am here to serve, not to exalt myself. I'm here to bless people; some may never come back to honour me, but that's not the motive for service. The moment you see that you want to be specially recognized for what you're doing, know that you're already moving in the wrong direction. Bring yourself back to the place of service. None of us can serve more than Jesus served, to the point where he laid down his life for us.

5

Managing Pressure From Followers

God's government is not democratic. This message is challenging in this part of the world where we have a democracy and the freedom to express ourselves. When God chooses a leader, He is not looking for someone who will necessarily be popular, but rather someone who is willing to be obedient to His will so that He can work through them to bring about His purposes. Good leaders should seek feedback from the people they are leading. I prefer not to use the term "followers," as we are all leaders and followers in various aspects of our lives.

In the case of Abraham, God said that He knew Abraham would follow His ways and lead his family accordingly. Recently, I had a conversation with a husband from a family who had been part of our church. He informed me that they would be transitioning out of Cornerstone, but he wasn't seeking a blessing or any guidance from me. Instead, he had decided after he asked his children which church they wanted to attend. The children obviously picked a different church because their friends were there. I was shocked to hear this because it seemed like the family had decided without God's guidance. It's like me asking the church members what theme they want for the year. People go to their friends for something that has to do with their destiny and completely ignore God. Unfortunately, this is a common occurrence among Christians, where people rely on the advice of others instead of seeking God's direction.

When God chooses someone to lead, He wants someone who is confident and bold enough to be a vessel for His will. This does not mean that the leader should be autocratic, as God wants His people to use their strengths to lead in different areas. Even in Moses' leadership, when he chose skilled individuals, he did not micromanage them; instead, he allowed them to lead in their areas of strength. God has absolute responsibility for making decisions, and He desires to call the shots. Therefore, any leader who is not bold enough to allow God to guide their decisions will likely not last long. For instance, I could tell a leader that God said from today everyone must enter through a specific door. A fearful leader might then consult with the members of the ushering ministry who enforced this rule and ask for their opinion on what I said. However, this would not be the same message; one was an instruction, while the other was a suggestion. That's why this topic is crucial and critical because it's not easy to tell people things that even you don't understand.

I can only imagine how Abraham felt when he went home and told Sarah they were leaving his father's house. If she asked where they were going, Abraham would say, "I don't know, but I heard a voice saying Abraham, leave your father's house and go to a place I will show you. Sarah, pack your things. Lot, come with us." It was not an easy conversation, but asking questions was essential. For example, "Abraham, where are you taking us? Where are we going?" It takes a bold leader to admit they don't know where they're going, but God said they are going, so they must begin the journey.

As a leader, there will come a time when you must choose whom you will obey, whether God or the people you lead. People may pressure them to do what they have not been asked to do, either actively or passively. Active pressure is when someone protests, saying, "Nope, I don't think it makes sense, and I don't think I'm going to do it." Passive pressure is when the subordinates are quiet when the leader speaks, and when asked if there are any questions, they say no, but it's clear they are not receiving the message. If you are a public speaker or lead worship in a ministry, you have been taught to observe your audience. Sometimes you speak or sing, and it's evident that the audience or members have completely tuned out.

Now let's examine some examples of people who experienced pressure as leaders and managed it well and others who did not manage it well and how it impacted their leadership.

JOB

One person who managed pressure well is Job. Let's look at Job 2:7-10; In this passage, Job's wife, who was one of his followers, pressured him to curse God and die. However, He was able to resist and refused to do it. In many cases, a church might split, and the Pastor would decide to destroy the church in the process. I have studied that the pressure to behave in that way usually comes from the Pastor's wife. It's important to note that while we have examples in scripture where women like Eve and Sarah put pressure on their spouses and led them astray, we also have examples of women like Abigail and Esther who led their husbands in the right direction. Ultimately, as a leader, you must be careful about who you listen to, as you will be responsible for the actions they cause you to take.

JESUS

Another example of someone who managed pressure well is Jesus. In Luke 9:51-56, Jesus was being compared to Elijah, and it was said that if Elijah had been disrespected, He would not have allowed Himself to be humiliated that way. A leader who lacks self-confidence will feel the need to overcompensate and show the people that they are greater than Elijah. The pressure came on Jesus to do something He wouldn't have ordinarily done, but He didn't allow Himself to be misled in the wrong direction. A time will come when you will have to choose whether to obey what God has said to you or what people are saying to you. Many times, people will not be there when God speaks to them. From a ministry perspective, I am fully responsible for what goes on at CCCG; whether I do it directly or someone else does it, I am fully responsible.

We had someone who moved from our church to Montreal and wanted to stay connected and find a new church. He didn't find what he was looking for and was imploring me to start another branch in Montreal. It looked like God was moving, but I said no because God had not spoken to me. He brought it up again, and I told him that if he kept doing that, I wouldn't speak to him as much anymore because God had not spoken to me about that matter. When things are peaceful and moving smoothly, it means that God's hands are in the situation. Many use the phrase "God spoke to me," but just because I can do something does not mean I have to do it, nor does it mean that God was asking me to do it. To some people, that would look like progress.

When you are doing things that people like, you may not experience pressure, but the moment God asks you to do something that people will not accept or understand, the pressure will begin to come. People will bring all kinds of opposition because they feel like your idea will bring them all kinds of inconvenience. I've learned that once God has spoken, I've already moved. It's up to you if you follow, but if you don't, it's also up to you. People will always do what they want to do anyway, but as leaders, we have to make sure that if God is the one raising us and has selected us, He is allowed to call the shots. This is extremely important. God is not democratic. When He gives instructions, He's not asking for people's opinions. When God says something, even I do not have an opinion. That's the way I am trying to live my life. When God is the one that says what to do, I'd rather have it His way than try another way. When God was directing the children of Israel out of Egypt, He didn't ask the children of Israel what path to take. The moment the pillar of fire was moving, they had to move; otherwise, they would have missed the way.

Let me pause and ask us a question. Have you ever experienced pressure from the people you're leading? Absolutely! It's a normal thing. Parents, of course, many times tell their kids to go to sleep, and the children ask them why. Now the parent has to explain that it's better for them to sleep earlier than not. The kids feel like they know better.

MOSES & AARON

Exodus 32:1-29. What kind of leader was Moses? What kind of leader was Aaron? Aaron was insecure as a leader because he was easily swayed by what the people had asked him to do. It didn't even appear as though he was showing any resistance here. It was almost as if he had wanted to do that, and he had been dreaming of that day when he would take over from his younger brother, Moses. He didn't even say that he wanted to go think about it. Right there, he came up with a solution. I can only imagine how difficult it was for Aaron, especially for Mariam. These people probably saw Moses being born, and now he was trying to be this big, powerful prophet. It would have taken the grace of God for them to support Moses and not try to usurp his authority. Moses was spoken about in a very disparaging way, but Aaron didn't say anything to defend him. Moses understood that it was better for the people to fall into his hands than into God's hands. One of the worst things that can happen to you is if you offend a Pastor or any child of God, and the person tells you that they would just leave you in God's hands. If that person is truly walking with God, please beg them to forgive you.

CONFIDENCE IN LEADERSHIP

Confidence is crucial. Aaron was a leader who lacked confidence. Confidence is one of the main factors that is needed to make a leader succeed. What does confidence look like? It looks like taking ownership of your actions, ownership of your speech, ownership of your ideas, and taking ownership of everything that emanates from you. If we juxtapose that with Adam and Eve, God just wanted Adam to take ownership of the fact that he also contributed to their fall, but Adam never did. He deflected to Eve. Only God knows what the world would have looked like if Adam had taken responsibility and said, "Lord, I'm sorry. I shouldn't have listened to that advice. She wasn't there when you gave me the instruction that we should not eat from the tree. It's my fault, and I am sorry."

HOW TO BUILD CONFIDENCE

Take Inventory of Your Strengths

You lack confidence because you focus more on other people's strengths than yours. It is as simple as that. If you take inventory by sitting down and listing out the strengths you have, you will come to the conclusion that you are not that bad. If your attention is on other people, then obviously, you cannot be a confident leader. You'll always tell yourself that someone is better than you. When you give suggestions, you won't be sure about them, so you backtrack. Other people teach or preach one way, and then they turn and look at people's faces to gauge the value of what they're saying. If they see that the reception is not there from the people, the leader would backtrack, feeling intimidated.

Remind Yourself That God Selected You

That's what David told Michal, his wife. "It is the God who selected me instead of your father Saul, that's the person I'm dancing to today," Paul told Timothy the same thing when he told him not to let anyone despise his youth. It's very clear. Let's use age as an example. You will never be the right age to lead. You'll either be too young or too old. There is no perfect age. God said the same thing to Jeremiah. It has nothing to do with age. At the age of 12, Jesus was in the temple, questioning the leaders. It's all about confidence. Remind yourself of how God selected you and that He was intentional.

Surround Yourself With People Who Validate You

You need to surround yourself with people who will give you feedback in a constructive and non-hypocritical way. Aaron lacked confidence, and he was also covetous. When Moses was going up to meet with God, he didn't just leave and go up on the mountain. No, that would have been irresponsible. He handed them over to Aaron and Mariam. For Aaron to turn around and not even respond to the people was a sign of covetousness and rebellion. He wanted what Moses had.

There is a difference between flattery and good feedback. Sometimes people praise you, and they never correct you. That approach is imbalanced. Which means it is hypocritical. If you find yourself in a position where you're covetous, it's a very dangerous place to be. Most likely, what has happened is, that you've lost track of your own relevance. All you need to do is to relocate, find, and realign with your purpose.

Let's say someone has been called to be a music minister in the church, and suddenly because they are sitting under a Pastor that preaches very well, this anointed music minister begins to fantasize about preaching the Word, just like the Pastor they are under. They have lost their way already or are losing their way. If they are not careful, they will lose their calling and struggle to be second best to somebody else.

How do you know you're becoming covetous? When somebody else is being appreciated and it is affecting you, you know you've been stung by covetousness. That's what happened to Judas when he saw how Jesus was treated. He was angry and thought, "Why are we doing all this for Him." What would you do if you ever found yourself in that situation? Repent and ask God to realign your heart. Covetousness is dangerous because it is a sin of the heart and can be hidden, just like pride. It is still seen by God. I like to watch when a lady comes into the room and observes the other ladies, you would hardly find one that looks and says that they have nice shoes. They would just keep it to themselves.

Build a Strong Relationship With God

Aaron did not have a relationship with God. Wherever Moses went, Joshua was there. When you realize that a leader under you loves to spend more time with the people you are leading than with God, that is a dangerous place to be. If you read the previous chapters, you can see that God had spoken to Aaron multiple times, but if you look at Aaron's response, you will see that he did not know God; otherwise, he would not have been so willing to make a golden calf for the Israelites. As a leader, you must have a relationship with God first. For example, Jesus prayed the whole night before he selected his leaders the next day. However, he still selected Judas, but it had to happen because it was prophesied.

Relinquish Fear

Aaron was a fearful leader. Lacking confidence is not the same as being fearful. Have you ever been in a situation where you were so afraid that you didn't even know what you were saying? Can you estimate how many people came to Aaron for him to make another god? According to church history, millions of people left Egypt, with tribal leaders and leaders of families appointed to lead and watch over specific groups of people in the multitude. Out of 3 million people, perhaps a few hundred thousand people approached Aaron, say, one percent of 3 million people, that is 30,000. The Bible said that the Israelites were a stiff-necked people, so they must have pondered the thought for a while before approaching Aaron aggressively. If you do not have boldness, words can cause a person to begin to falter.

All Elijah heard was just a message from one woman, Jezebel, and the great prophet ran away. If you remember the story of Jacob, his sons, and his daughter Dina, they travelled and got to Shechem. The Bible says that Dina, one of Jacob's daughters, decided to play around with the other daughters of the woman in the land. One of the princes saw her and sexually assaulted her. In the process, he fell in love with her. Jacob's sons heard the story and got angry. They set up a ploy and a great deception, encouraging the men of the land to circumcise themselves as they were going to give Dina to them. When a man is circumcised, they are incapacitated for days. So the men did that, and on the third day, at the height of their pain, Jacob's sons, led by Simeon, came and killed them all. Jacob did not say anything because he knew his sons until he was about to die. So imagine tens of thousands of people like Simeon or Levi. It would have taken boldness and confidence.

When Moses appeared on the scene and people saw how he operated, they knew he was not afraid for his life. Jesus said we should not fear a man who can only kill the body but fear God, who can kill both the body and destroy the soul. The fear of men is a snare and an entrapment. How should Aaron have responded? Aaron should have reminded the people of what God had done for them. They saw the Red Sea part and all the miracles of God. In Exodus 14:13, it says that the people were afraid at the Red Sea. Moses told the people to relax and not to fear, but a few verses later, God asked Moses why he was afraid and told him to tell the people to move forward. However, as a leader, he told the people to relax because he saw that they were discouraged.

The same thing happened to David. When they got back to Ziklag, they saw that their children, wives, and possessions were taken. The mighty men were crying, and the Bible says they wanted to stone David. What did David do? He strengthened himself in the Lord, even though he was distraught. David said to Abiathar the priest, "...*Please, Bring the ephod,*" (1 Samuel 30:7) and he consulted God. He never blamed the people for getting angry and being down. Blaming the people is what followers do, but we are leaders.

Confidence in Times of Pressure

You have five types of followers based on the way people respond to change:

1. **Innovators**
2. **Early Adopters**
3. **Middle Adopters**
4. **Late Adopters**
5. **Laggards**

Even though all these people gathered, most likely, there were some ringleaders. That's usually how it is in crowds: one, two, or three people were stirring all those people up. As a leader, you need to understand that the devil will try to deceive you and make it feel like everyone is against you when there are only a few people. Once you crush the head of the snake, everyone else will be quieted.

Let's look at another character called Saul. In 1 Samuel 13:1-15, we see another leader who succumbed to the pressure of followers, and in the process, he lost his throne, dynasty, and leadership. What are the similarities between Saul and Aaron? In the above scripture, Samuel gave Saul a timeframe for when he would arrive. However, Samuel didn't show up at the appointed time, and Saul went ahead to perform Samuel's task. Was that partly Samuel's fault? No. What should Saul have done? He should have waited. Aaron and Saul had many similarities: covetousness, lack of boldness, fearfulness, and no relationship with God.

On the other hand, David had a relationship with God even when there was a prophet called Nathan. Throughout these passages, there is no evidence that Saul prayed to God, but we can find many records of David praying to God.

Why are we saying all these things? Pressure will come when you're leading people. Why must pressure come? Because you are a leader. God spoke to you in many cases when he didn't speak to them. They will get confidence once they see results, but it was you God spoke to about it, or you perceived what God was saying. It is not all the time there will be a consensus among the people you are leading before you take a step. Don't always look for agreement from everybody before you take a step. That is a function of confidence.

Take Responsibility

Are there times when you will make mistakes as a leader? Absolutely. You should also own up to your mistakes, but there will not always be a consensus. In Saul's case, his focus was on the people, not on God. Are you a leader who gives excuses? Can you accept responsibility for deficiencies in your team? The people who give you the most pressure are those who don't have faith. Leadership is all about moving people from one point to another point, and it takes faith to see into the future. When I see myself around people who don't believe in a vision, I prepare my heart for the opposition. And it's not that they're doing it intentionally, but because they don't have faith, they have to question you. And when there's no faith, all that remains is rationalization, using the head (or common sense) to analyze every situation.

As a ministry, we had to renovate the new church we purchased, the leaders knew what was in our account. It didn't make any sense. However, we have great leaders who didn't raise those types of questions. If we had leaders with no faith, there would have been opposition all around. May God surround you with people who are full of faith in the name of Jesus! People can only be helpful and useful once they are led by God. They will become a thorn in your flesh when they are out of God's leading. Saul was judging his success based on all the battles he had won. Therefore, you could tell that he would end up where he ended up. He wasn't about the people. It was the throne that was his focus. Nobody is indispensable except the Holy Spirit.

I've learned as a leader never to put my trust in any human being. Don't learn these things by experience; learn them by receiving wisdom from scriptures. There was a time when the people came to Jesus, and they wanted to make him king. He knew their hearts that it was because He gave them bread and food. He ran away from them. When the pressure comes, can you manage it?

DEALING WITH DISCOURAGEMENT & DISAPPOINTMENT

Before the church started, I went to God and asked many questions. The Bible says, *"For which of you, intending to build a tower, does not sit down first and count the cost, whether he has enough to finish it—"* (Luke 14:28). So, one of my questions was how I could last in the ministry because ministry is not a sprint, it is a marathon. Among other things, God said to watch out for discouragement and disappointment. I asked God, "What do you mean?" He replied, "Disappointment is when you have the wrong expectation." He then showed me great men and women who fell, not because of the devil, but because of the wrong expectations they had of people. When people disappointed them, they were heartbroken, and that's when the enemy was able to come and harass them.

Elijah was heartbroken and disappointed because he expected a revival and many great things to go back to the way they were after the fire came down from heaven. However, the next day, he received a message that Jezebel wanted to kill him, and disappointment took hold. Discouragement is when the result you get is much lower than what you were expecting.

During our first Come and See event, we were excited and rented a space outside of the church at the time. We fasted and prayed, saw visions – both man-made and God-made - and rented equipment. It was a big space! That day, we came, but not many people came to see. Four people gave their lives to Christ, and we had to encourage them to do so. After the event, we began to pack up and move our stuff back to the church. I noticed some of the leaders were visibly discouraged, so I called them and advised them that this is how the ministry usually starts in the beginning. Nothing great starts big; everything great starts small. A time will come when stadiums won't be able to contain our gatherings. Right now, there are people in the Bahamas who consider CCCG their home church. Our basic leadership classes now include members from different countries: Bahamas, Canada, France, the United States and many others. God already prepared my heart for discouragement.

Some time ago, we had night prayers. Our preparation was very vigorous. God spoke prophetic words, words of knowledge, and advised that someone would begin to receive strange favour. A man in the service received it, and after the service, he came to me and said that someone had immediately called him and given him an envelope with $200. Immediately after he shared that with me, the devil began to suggest that it should have been me who received the money. All I said was, "Shut up." I could only do that because my heart was prepared for discouragement. To carry the vision, you need to be confident with the vision you carry. Not confident in the people but in the vision. Anyone can come, and anyone can go. For some, God didn't send them; the devil sent them. For others, God sent them, but only for a little while. For others, God sent them, and they will be with you for a long time. In order to shield yourself from pressure, know who you are serving, who called you, and who appointed you. It's not the people; it is God, the Authority.

KNOW THE INSTRUCTIONS GIVEN

If Abraham had not succumbed to the pressure from Sarah, maybe there would not have been issues with the many terrorist groups we see in the world today. Years ago, I was serving in the youth ministry at a different ministry, and another Pastor was going to get married in Kenya. The Pastor made me the lead, and she became my assistant so I could learn from her. I remember there was fierce opposition from the youth leaders I used to serve with. They were serving alongside me, and now I was the one heading the ministry.

One day, I had enough of it. I went to the head Pastor and advised him of what they were doing and how they were trying to frustrate everything he was doing. I asked him to go and warn them about their behaviour. He said to me at that moment, "I can go and warn them, but they would only listen to you because of me. My advice to you is to ask God to validate your leadership." I didn't agree with his words at the time but said okay. However, by the time I got home, what he said made sense to me, and I prayed that prayer as recommended by the Pastor.

We used to go to events and different conferences, I remember that there was a ringleader of the group. She would ask me tricky questions and inquire what I thought about that specific issue. One of those days, she did that, and I began to feel how Jesus felt when the Pharisees kept trying to pin him down with a specific question. Then I began to speak, and everyone around me started to realize that what I was saying was true. One after the other, they began to submit and realized that God actually put me in that position. I remember I was teaching one day, and this lady leading the opposition against me walked in. I remember God opened my eyes, and I saw her underneath a dark cloud. The dark cloud was following her as she was coming in. The Holy Spirit advised me to address it after she sat down.

After she sat down, I asked her to stand beside me. She came reluctantly and with an attitude. I told the congregation that when she was coming in, I saw a dark cloud, and everyone should pray for her. As we all prayed, I noticed her eyes were open, and she was just watching everyone. The next day, on Sunday, we had our normal service. While I was heading home, she called me. She called me "Pastor Emmanuel," which was strange because she had never called me that before. She said that she had gone to the head Pastor's office, and as soon as she entered, he looked at her and said a dark cloud was following her. I started smiling. She then continued to tell me that she remembered what I told her the previous day and kept asking me for directions. From that day on, she never disrespected me again. Sometimes, the pressure is not because the people are wicked, but maybe because they're weak or they don't understand. As long as you are confident as a leader, that's what matters.

DO WHAT HAS BEEN GIVEN YOU TO DO

Not everyone will accept you as a leader; you need to be comfortable with that. No matter the miracles you do or the results you are getting, know that not everybody will accept you as a leader. That's what happened to Jesus. Just focus on those who have accepted you and ensure you minister to them and lead them appropriately. Ordinarily, Saul's reaction and decision-making were justified, but more is usually expected of us as leaders. So, in that case, his response was appropriate. Juxtapose that with Gideon, who started with 32,000 soldiers, and after God's sifting process, he was left with 300 people. Gideon was fearful, but he trusted and obeyed God. Saul, on the other hand, disobeyed God. God wants everybody to be a leader, but the truth is not everybody can pay the price to be a leader.

SET THE RIGHT EXPECTATIONS

Faith comes by hearing and hearing the Word of God. Our expectations should be based on what God has said. If God has not spoken expressly, then we should be cautious. Once God has spoken, we can put our all into it. So, the right approach is to follow what God has said either directly to us or through His Word. The best way to know is to ask Him questions. If God says something, praise Him. But if He has not said anything specific in an area, don't say that God has failed you. We must keep in mind that there is a stage in our walk with God where the devil cannot openly deceive us with lies, but he can deceive us with half-truths. This is what the devil tried to do with Jesus. He told Him to jump and that God would cause His angels to keep watch over Him. That was a half-truth.

When David went to bring the Ark of the Covenant into the city of David, it seemed like a good thing. But why did God kill Uzzah in that account? God killed Uzzah because He had told Israel how to carry the Ark, it had to be carried on the shoulders of the people. Instead, they made a new technology to carry the Ark, which violated God's principles. As a result, when they got to a specific threshing floor of Nacon, the Ark wanted to fall. Someone put his hand there to prevent it from falling. At that point, God was already angry because they violated His principles, so God killed Uzzah for touching the Ark. However, the next time they were going to transport the Ark, David inquired of God, and he did it properly. Every few steps along the journey, they sacrificed to God.

TRUST HAS TO BE EARNED

You don't just get trust because you're a leader; you earn it. When followers see over time that when you say something, you mean it, they will begin to trust you. They will put you in a class of your own as someone who follows through and is honest. Rise up and lead. The world is looking for bold leaders.

OVERCOMING SYSTEMIC OPPRESSION IN LEADERSHIP

I will briefly discuss two aspects of systemic oppression in leadership: **Women** and **Visible Minorities.** Coming from a place of oppression can be an uphill task, but the truth is that all it takes is one person who is willing to swim against the tide and pay the price for everybody else. If you come from a place of historical disadvantage, understand that you can change people's perspectives if willing to pay the price. It is not going to be easy.

Women

Take Gloria Copeland, for example. She was speaking at a conference, and a man came to her and kept addressing her as 'brother Copeland' because he did not believe that women should be allowed to speak publicly. So if she had allowed that to bug her, we wouldn't have had her books to study. So you don't know what you're losing when you decide to sit down and allow a few people to oppress you, mentally especially. Slavery has not ended; it's just the physical slavery that ended. People are still trying to enslave others mentally, in the workplace, community, and in many other areas.

Visible Minorities

I know what it is like professionally in different circles. I hardly pay attention in those scenarios, but many people do. In many cases, I am the only dark-skinned person in the room. If I pay attention to the people who don't trust me, my confidence will be attacked. I know who I am and where I came from. No one just handed me opportunities. I thank God for His favour, but I am educated. I have things to say, and my mind is working well. So I go into the room with that boldness and audacity. You can roll your eyes and do anything you want to do, but at the end of the day, I have the right to sit at the table, and I've earned my seat. Eventually, some people will come on my side, and others will never because they have that inherent belief that because of my race or gender, I do not have the right to speak. That is their own opinion.

ALLOW GOD TO VALIDATE YOU

Whatever you are and wherever you are, if God has put you in a place of authority, take the lead. Leadership has nothing to do with age. Some people will despise you for your age. Allow God to validate your leadership. Paul said to Timothy not to let anyone despise his youth. If you don't rise up now and begin to lead, and you allow other people to deceive you, you will get to the point where you'll realize that you've become too old. But that will not be your portion in Jesus' name!

6

Avoiding Burnout

There is something that happens when you keep exerting yourself continuously. You get to the point where it seems like you no longer know yourself. It can manifest physically, mentally, emotionally, and even spiritually. Suddenly, you find that you've reached a point where you are giving way more than you're receiving. You're already in a state of burnout. This is similar to a candle that is lit, giving light to others, but at its own expense. If it continues down that path, the next thing you know, the light continues to go down until it all melts away. It's also like soap, where you use it to help someone else stay clean, but the soap disintegrates with every use.

As a leader, you are giving out something every time you serve, speak, or counsel someone. Every time you stay on the phone with someone who is complaining, you're giving, and something is being taken away from you. For some in their workplaces as well, they're in a constant state of giving. You'll see a serious imbalance when you compare that with how much they are receiving. No wonder many people are never able to rise above situations. Many of us know that people who work out eat more or are supposed to eat more, or their system will break down. Imagine someone going to the gym and working six hours daily but only eating a salad. The person will suddenly pass out one day because they don't have the energy to sustain themselves. Their output is way more than their input.

The reward for good work is more work. When you are doing good, more things will be put on your plate. Sadly, as many leaders get promoted to do more, they don't consume more to match what they're giving. Suddenly, you get to a state where Pastors are committing suicide, people are leaving the faith, getting discouraged and disappointed in mass.

When we're burnt out, just like our physical bodies, as an individual, we are more susceptible to challenges. We can't respond to things the way we ought to respond to them. Isaiah 40:28 says that if you don't take definite steps as a leader, you will find it hard to be fresh. It's one of the things we enjoy to the glory of God at CCCG. When I discovered Isaiah 40:31, I told God that this was what I wanted – to soar with wings like an eagle, to walk and not be weary.

Let's say that you're using your phone, and it's fully charged. As you use it, your battery level begins to go down. Some people are smart enough to carry a charger. That's the story of the five wise virgins from scripture; they carried the extra oil. Some people leave their phones plugged in while they are using it. Spiritually, that's the state I have decided to be in; where I am giving, but I am also receiving way more. This allows me to always have fresh oil, according to Psalm 92:10. Two important things to be aware of:

1. **It's Possible to Get Burnt Out**
2. **Incorporate Steps Into Your Routine to Prevent Burnout**

When do you usually fill up your gas tank while driving? Some people do it at a quarter tank, some at half tank and some when your tank is almost empty. If we're not careful, we might treat our spiritual lives the same way we treat filling up our gas tank. Once, I met someone whose spouse encouraged him to meet with me. By the time we spoke, he was breaking down in tears. That was a red flag. Such individuals are often those who give a lot of themselves to others. Many of our parents raised us while burnt out for decades. It's no surprise that they cursed or abused us, even unintentionally. How many times did your parents take a vacation on their own to recharge? Most likely, you can't recall any. And even if it happened, it was infrequent. If we want to thrive and stand strong, this isn't how it's supposed to be.

Numerous leaders, workers, Pastors, and administrators are burnt out, yet they keep going. They haven't realized that they're no longer adding value; they're taking away value from others because they're misrepresenting the faith due to burnout. Only God can continue without becoming weary or weak. As human beings, we are not surprised that our stomachs growl when we're hungry. We'll feel hungry, especially if we haven't eaten in a whole day. As leaders, we almost feel guilty for needing to be filled.

SIGNS OF BURNOUT

Heightened Fear

You become easily frightened. Things that usually wouldn't scare you suddenly do because your mind knows it can't handle anything else.

Anger

You become short-tempered over small things and blow them out of proportion. Going back to the man I met, something small occurred, and his reaction was exaggerated. So I suggested he take some time off to rest because he was clearly burnt out. Anyone can step on your toes, and you'll dismiss it, but when you're burnt out, it's World War 3. And you know it's not your typical behaviour. These are signs that you've gone beyond your limit and need to take a break to recharge yourself.

Prayerlessness

When you are unable to pray the way you normally do, read the word as you normally do or worship, it is a sign that you are sick spiritually, just as losing the appetite for food is a sign of physical sickness. When you experience burnout, you lose your appetite for spiritual things, and even though you know that you should pray, your mouth is not willing to pray. I have been there before and never want to be there again because that is not a good place to be. Being empty and burnt out limits how much value we can add.

Disillusionment

This is one of the most dangerous states of burnout, where you question everything, such as why we worship God or if it matters anymore. Being disillusioned means being farther away from reality, just like someone in a coma is alive but not really alive. The enemy can keep people busy and make them do many tasks, but when they are burnt out, they start to question the point of doing anything: "Is there even a point to what we're doing, or is God even real?" When you are burnt out, nothing seems to matter anymore. It's like a phone with a low battery that stops all functionalities except the basic one until it is recharged. When a person is in a state of burnout, they may even deny their faith, which is the height of it.

Deep Discouragement

This is a state of burnout where it becomes difficult to encourage someone. When you keep moving even though you are burnt out, you will keep making mistakes, it's like quicksand. The longer you go without addressing the burnout, the more mistakes you make, and the more those mistakes will validate your beliefs. The character we will be focusing on is Elijah in 1 Kings 19:1. In the previous chapter, Elijah brought about a revival and killed 450 prophets of Baal, but in chapter 19, he saw a letter and ran. Elijah was burnt out. If he was not burnt out, he would have had the ability to fight back. After the intensive ministry activity in the previous chapter, Elijah did not take time off to recharge and get refreshed, which made him lose his place as a prophet.

Many leaders have resigned from leadership positions because of burnout. Not because they faced challenges, which we all do, but because they faced a challenge when they were burnt out. When a person is burnt out, they may overreact, and their temptations will become stronger, which is a bad state to be in. Burnout can also be when a good person does something bad and then looks back and wonders what made them do that. As an individual, I know when I need a retreat, when I need to receive from my spiritual authority, and when I need to rest. In this race we are running, it's not everybody who starts that finishes the race.

There was a series on Netflix on Bishop Carlton. He was a particular Bishop in the United States that Oral Roberts himself mentored. Many people said all kinds of things with regard to his potential. A very well-spoken man! Before long, he denied the faith. Prior to that, he brought a new doctrine to the body, stating that Jesus Christ was not the only way to the Father. According to his story, he watched a TV ad after losing a loved one, and a voice told him, "Would this kind of a person go to hell if they didn't hear the gospel?" That's when he told himself that God was not that wicked and you didn't need to believe in Jesus to go to heaven. Bishops called him and asked him to state his case and show evidence from scripture. However, he continued down that path, leading one of the largest churches in the US.

That church is currently down to a handful of people. He's still holding on to the idea as of today. Not everybody who starts the race ends the race. This topic for me is very important. The Bible says, *"Let he who stands take heed, lest he falls."* (1 Corinthians 10:12) Just because you went to the buffet yesterday doesn't mean that you will remain full forever. After a major victory, you don't even feel like reading the Bible because you remember everything from Bible studies! I have seen quite a lot. Some people think that because they were at a powerful night prayer, it would carry them for a whole year. That's deceiving yourself. All it takes is one counseling call where you're on the phone with someone who complains for one hour, and your 'battery' begins to go down. This will not be your portion in Jesus' name!

CAUSES OF BURNOUT

One-Sided Ministrations

Ministering to others but not receiving ministration. I have observed a common behaviour among instrumentalists in different ministries. They think their role is solely to play music and fail to listen to the word. After playing, they leave and go about their own business. It is no wonder that their lives sometimes take a downward turn. I was taught early on that when I preach, I am ministering to others, but I can also receive my own ministration by paying attention to what is being said. Many people tell others but refuse to listen. Even if you can quote scripture back-to-back, you still need to be ministered to. At one time, God had me speak with some of the social workers in CCCG and inquire whether they understood the nature of their careers. In social work, they teach them to do self-care.

Intensive Ministry Activity

A significant emotionally draining activity or occurrence. In the case of Elijah, he experienced numbers one and two. Jesus had experienced number three. The death of a loved one, a breakup, or a close friend moving away are examples of significant, emotionally draining activities that can quickly lead to burnout. When John the Baptist was beheaded, Jesus took time off to go to the wilderness alone. After feeding the multitude, He told the disciples to go ahead of Him so He could stay alone and inquire of the Lord. After that, He returned, recharged, and even walked on water to meet His disciples.

Functioning Outside Your Calling

Constantly walking outside of your area of calling can lead to serious burnout. The opposite of this is one of my secrets. When you do what you are called to do, God puts in place a natural system that will keep you fired up.

HOW TO STAY RECHARGED

Worship

Just listening to music does not mean you are worshipping. If you are not getting the desired result, pause what you're doing and ask questions. Once, while driving home from work, the Holy Spirit asked me if I knew why the Lord neither sleeps nor slumbers. When the Holy Spirit asks questions, He knows I don't have the answer. He answered and said, "Have you not read that 24/7, anointed worship is going on in heaven? If you can ensure your environment is filled with anointed worship constantly, you will hardly get tired." As you grow older, you'll realize that energy is an important resource.

Regarding the choice of music, wherever the song came from is where it will take you when you listen to it. If it came from God, it will take you to God. We cannot be in sin and ask for grace to abound. I am not judging anybody, but we need to know and understand these things. There are two facets of worship (Revelations 4):

1. **Worshiping God on the Throne**
2. **Validating God**

In Revelation 4:1-11, we see there is worship that is given, and there is worship that is received. This is why you cannot be recharged if you're hanging around people who are always pulling you down. Same cycle. All you hear from them are your mistakes. Did you hear that God made any mistakes while he created man? No, nothing like that. No matter how anointed you are, if you stay around people who will pull you down, your anointing will begin to decrease. I avoid those people like the plague. I minister to those people if I need to, but I don't hang around them. What God has given me is precious to me.

Remain Where You Are Loved

Jesus Christ of Nazareth demonstrated something very important that we can learn from: He was never far away from the house of Mary, Martha, and Lazarus, where He ministered to many different people. The Bible never told us that He visited some of His disciples' homes, but we know that He visited Peter because He healed Peter's mother-in-law. The Bible never told us if He went to Judas' house or anybody else's; if He did, it didn't find it noteworthy to mention. However, the Bible recorded at least three times when Jesus went to the house of Mary, Martha, and Lazarus. Why? Because that was where He was being loved, and the red carpet was always rolled out for Him. He was treated like a king in their house. Before He made any ministry-defining move, He would go there. For example, before He went to die on the cross, He was at their house. You need to find your own Mary, Martha, and Lazarus.

For some people, they might not be in your home or within your family, it's the place where you long to go, and you are treated like a king, where you are loved and accepted. There are some places you go where all they want is to take things from you, and that is okay when you know ahead of time so you can be prepared. There are some other places where they want to love you. You hear some leaders saying that it is lonely at the top, but I am not lonely because of these principles that are practiced. Apply these principles as often as possible, and when you do, your life won't be the same.

There is worship that you give to God, and there are validations and affirmations that you receive back as well. When you genuinely spend time with God, in many cases, you receive affirmations back from Him. Why did God say to Jesus that Jesus was His beloved son in whom He was well pleased? Because Jesus needed it. Jesus knew this already, but He needed to hear it. Are we perfect? No! But we are all works in progress.

Personal Worship

Worship can be the songs you sing to God, it can also be the words you say to God, it doesn't need to be a song. It can be poems like in the book of Psalms. The worship songs that are the most special are the words you coin personally to God. How would you feel if the person you're married to or dating, in a Godly relationship, wrote you a letter and showed you where they got the poem from because they didn't want to plagiarise? Maybe they meant the things that they said, but you're shocked that they didn't have anything to say from their own heart. It's okay to sing other songs, but the best form of worship is what you personally say from your heart to God.

Search For Anointed Songs

Songs written by other people can take us to that place, but there's a place you get to in God where you turn off those worship songs because they become a distraction, where God wants to hear from you Himself. How would you know that the song you're listening to is anointed? While listening, study what is happening to you. There are many songs I hear people singing and playing, but I can't sense anything anointed in them. The words are good, and the technicality in the instrumentals is great, but the touch of the Holy Spirit is missing.

When I listen to a song and sense God's anointing, I add it to my anointed song playlist. You don't wait until you're totally down on groceries before you go grocery shopping. Those songs should already be there in your arsenal when you need them. Some people are taken to the presence of God by instrumentals, not songs with words; for others, it's not just any instrumentals, but specific instruments.

God used David to introduce many of these instruments into the world. That is why the Israelites had to listen to specific songs or sounds of music before they went into battle because those sounds took them to a specific atmosphere in God that would energize them for the battle.

For some people, it's different kinds of drum beats, while for others, it could be the piano, guitar, trumpet, saxophone, or other instruments. This is why I encourage the members of CCCG to quickly dominate their bodies, so they can begin to explore the deeper things in God. You need to go on this expedition yourself. When Abraham, Isaac, and Jacob got to specific places where God had spoken to them, they would build an altar there. On the demonic side, this is practiced way more than among Christians. They don't just settle in any place. Once they sense energy in a place, that's when they put up their flag. They use certain animals and items to perform their incantations because of the energy they carry, the energy that God has put in those things.

When you listen to worship songs, you don't always have to sing along with them. Just agreeing with it will cause the songs to work for you. You can simply have it playing in the background at work, at home, or in your vehicle, and it would still take you to that place in God. Worship is an excellent way to recharge spiritually.

Meditating on the Word of God

This is not just looking for any Scripture in the Bible; it's more specific. These are the Scriptures that God has spoken to you through in the past; those Scriptures that have come alive and set you ablaze before. All believers who truly pay attention will have those types of Scriptures. They could be the Scriptures that God used to communicate His vision for your life, to lead you to Christ, or to reveal something notable.

There was a particular year in a different Ministry I attended that used to have a Bible reading month. The church encouraged people to read the whole Bible that month, so I started reading with them that year. I couldn't go past Genesis 1: 1-3 for about three months. God kept speaking to me from those verses, and they still form the basis of everything I do today. When I was reading that, the Holy Spirit asked me one question: What challenges did God go through in the beginning, and what challenges did He tackle first? There were three main challenges:

1. **Darkness**
2. **The Earth was Without Form.**
3. **It was Empty.**

The first challenge He tackled was 'light'. Therefore, the Lord said to me never to go into anything without getting 'revelation' or 'understanding'. Anyone starting out in ministry, a business, a school, or anything must get revelation first.

Next, God tackled the form. When you're building a house, you don't add furniture when the frame has not been put up. When I was leading the youth ministry in another ministry, I asked God to bring people and send souls. He asked me to stop. He asked me which leaders would be able to support in caring for the people. It is way more difficult to bring former believers back than new believers. He instructed me to spend more time teaching the leaders and equipping them to lead the people. That's why the Lord instructed me to begin leadership classes when Cornerstone Christian Church of God started.

Lastly, He dealt with the emptiness. He began to fill up the earth with animals, birds, and all those things. People are too impatient. They don't take the time to build a foundation, pillars, structure, and organization.

Rest & Relaxation

Some people need to understand that rest is not evil and that they are not of the devil simply because they need to sleep or take time to rest. On the other hand, there are people who need to understand that too much sleep is not productive. The focus should be on how productive you are when you are awake, not how many hours you slept. It's important to be practical and focus on getting results. When we talk about rest, knowing what relaxes you is essential. It could be reading a book, talking to a loved one, journaling, or watching documentaries. In Genesis 2, God worked for six days and rested on the 7th day. Sometimes, we have been taught that resting is evil, but the Word of God can help us understand the importance of rest.

For some people, a change of scenery helps them to rest. My wife and I often book hotels in different parts of the city because our assignment doesn't allow us to go on vacations. However, vacations can help to calm us down. We must ask ourselves if we truly feel refreshed after returning from vacation. Knowing what works for you is essential because some people need a vacation after their vacation because they are not truly refreshed.

Resting in God means meditating on the Word of God, holding on to His promises, and allowing that to fill up your mind and thinking. It's important to take the time to rest and relax so that you can be productive when you are awake. The Bible teaches that we must labour to enter into God's rest. According to the Lord, the promise of God is the place of rest, regardless of our surroundings. Regarding rest and relaxation, when Elijah ran, the angel gave him food, which was evidence that Elijah lacked sleep and food. While fasting has its place, there is a point where it can lead to burnout and a diminishing return. Instead, we must learn to enjoy the good things of life in a measured way without allowing them to become our god.

Some people believe that God does not want us to enjoy life, but Scripture says that He satisfies our mouths with good things. Jesus went to people's houses and ate with them, and Paul learned to be abound and abased, teaching us how to manage ourselves properly.

Praying in the Holy Spirit

As stated in Jude 1:20. While some may wonder how to pray without ceasing, it can be done by praying in the Spirit even while talking to others. Kenneth Copeland shared a story about learning to pray in the Spirit and how he felt like he was wasting his time until he realized the impact it had on others. When we do spiritual things, we do them by faith, not by our feelings.

Fasting

Fasting is another way to recharge, but it only accelerates the other things we do, such as prayer, meditation on the Word, and worship. It's not an end in itself but rather a means to an end.

When God initiates a fast, we will receive grace and not feel the impact of it. However, we can also initiate a fast, and God will honour it, as Ezra did in Ezra 7:14 when seeking God's guidance to cross over to a new location. If we have initiated the fast ourselves, we must hold on as long as we can endure. Let us quickly review a few reminders regarding how we should fast. Many of us come from diverse backgrounds in faith.

Some of us have been indoctrinated to believe that we must break our fast at 6:00 p.m. and that this is the specific time to break the fast. However, there is no place in scripture that gives us a specific time to break our fast. Leadership can decide on a specific time to break the fast, and that's acceptable. However, one should not say that the instruction was from God. When someone comes into your home, you have your own rules on where to keep your shoes and everything else, but that does not apply universally. In the denomination where I grew up, the acceptable times to break the fast were 12:00 p.m., 3:00 p.m., and 6:00 p.m. Breaking the fast at 4:00 p.m. was not permitted. However, when I meditated on the scriptures, I did not find all of those things there. I can follow those rules for myself if I wish, but as a Pastor, I cannot teach people those things unless God instructs us to do so in the Ministry. I must tell the people exactly what the Word of God says. For example, if you were seeking God in fasting and prayer about something and He spoke to you concerning that matter at 11:00 a.m., but you continue fasting until 6:00 p.m., why are you continuing? Unless you have another reason to fast, then you're good to break your fast. This is how religion begins to take over people's lives with rigid rules that do not lead anyone closer to God.

Refreshing Your Mind: Vision, Mission & Purpose

If you have not yet written down your vision, mission, and purpose, I encourage you to do so and meditate on them frequently. Sometimes, burnout can lead to disillusionment, so you must remind yourself why you are doing what you're doing. This is the power of renewing vows. It strengthens you for the journey ahead. This is why I recommend that people have retreats at least once a year. It is a time to renew certain things with God; your vision and your purpose. Not just planning for the year but also remaining centered on what God wants you to do. Habakkuk 2:2-4 emphasizes this point. A parent might want their child to be raised without watching TV for long hours. But as time passes, this vision fades away. It is because they do not revisit what they had initially set their minds on.

That's why, in every single service, we say our mission and vision because we truly mean it. The goal is to ensure that it permeates everything we do at CCCG: "Bringing restoration and transformation to all by teaching, preaching, and demonstrating the gospel of Jesus Christ." The more you look at it and declare it, the more you're strengthened by it if you believe it and pursue it to the best of your ability.

Listening to Anointed Messages

I heard a message by Apostle Casey Price from 1988, and I was excited by the power in his words. Not all messages are like 'ice cream,' where when you hear them, you get excited, but later on, you feel empty. Therefore, you need to locate anointed messages for yourself and keep them accessible. So, when you're feeling low, you can fill up your tank. Some people always feel tired, as if they're carrying the world's weight on their heads. Who will give you more if you're not faithful in the little that God has given you?

There was a time when I had two full-time contracts, was doing a Ph.D., renovating the church building, and leading my family. You'll see the results when you follow these procedures and principles in a disciplined way for recharging. Just as we know how to eat breakfast, lunch, and dinner to stay alive physically, we need certain things to stay alive spiritually. However, when you're stressed, even the devil will find it easy to defeat you, as was the case of Elijah. Therefore, drop the things you don't need to be involved in and scale down to focus on what God says you need to do. Seeing results will help validate what you're doing, and you can build up from there.

CLDR: Connect, Learn, Do, Rest

There are some things that I must do every day, and it's something that the Lord gave me called **'CLDR'**.

- 'C' - **'Connect'**: Connect with God and the people who love me.
- 'L' - **'Learn'**: Learn something new every day.
- 'D' - **'Do'**: Do something and add value.
- 'R' - **'Rest'**: Rest to me may be different from what rest is to you.

7

Running With The Vision

What is a vision? A vision is a picture that encapsulates the future you want to achieve. We hear a lot about vision boards these days. Like all other topics, pay close attention to learning these practical tools. If we want to succeed in every aspect of our lives, we must have a vision for it. The Bible says, "Without a vision, my people perish." This means that if there is any area of your life without a clear vision, you're most likely not succeeding in that area, whether it be relationships, academics, career, or anything else. For instance, if a student doesn't decide from the beginning that they want to get an A, it will be very difficult to achieve an A.

DISCIPLINE

A lot of what makes a leader is discipline. If you begin to understand all the work involved in ensuring that your life moves the way it's meant to, you realize that discipline is extremely necessary. For example, at Jeff Bezos' level, I can imagine what it takes to manage $190 billion dollars (as of 2021). Some people can't even manage their car by keeping it clean. Many people dream of success because they think about its entertainment aspect. For instance, Shaquille O'Neal said that he spent a million dollars in a matter of 30 minutes. Mike Tyson said at one point in his life, he owned 100 Bentleys. Don't judge these people because you don't know what you'll do if you are in their situation.

It takes a lot of discipline to succeed; anybody you see succeeding in any area is disciplined. Let me give you another example. Jeff Bezos said that for him, in his planning, he is ten years ahead, and his next-level managers are five years ahead. I heard Bishop Oyedepo of Winners Chapel say that they have planned 30 years in advance. And I was thinking to myself, "No wonder some people succeed." When I was much younger in my home country of Nigeria, people spoke about Mission 2020. I used to think that 2020 was so far away. Now we are many years ahead of that.

When my parents visited me, I came across some of my dad's old pictures. I saw how young he looked and told my wife that while everyone will surely grow old, it never looks like it at the moment. But one day in 2060, we will all have had some mileage. What am I saying? A future you don't plan for, you can never achieve. Running with a vision is taking responsibility for the future you want to see. We say many things, like "What will be will be" or "God is in full control," among other religious phrases. But if God says you will get a job or be the next Prime Minister, and you don't join a political party or follow the system that has been put in place, it won't happen.

THE IMPORTANCE OF A VISION

Why is a vision important for a leader? I said something in the book "Dream Like A Child; Execute Like A Pro", and someone challenged me on it. I said that when you're running with a vision, you're indestructible. Someone reached out to me and asked if I was really sure of what I said. It is one of the reasons why distractions are very deadly and dangerous.

STEPHEN & PAUL

Two examples in scripture are Stephen and Paul. Both of them were stoned in the course of their lifetime. Stephen died, but Paul stayed alive. What's the difference? Vision. Not anointing or power. The Bible says Stephen was full of the Holy Ghost and full of power, which is one of the reasons why he was selected as one of the deacons. The Bible also says Stephen did mighty wonders in the midst of the people, but he died when he was getting stoned (Acts 7:54-60). In contrast, Paul didn't die when they stoned him (Acts 14:19-20). Philippians 1:21-26 explains why Paul couldn't die: he wasn't ready to go, so he 'chose' to remain. Stephen was stoned, but the stones did not kill him. Stones cannot kill a spirit-filled person, nor can bullets, sicknesses, or anything else. What kills people is when they decide to die, which is why they call it 'giving up the ghost.' The pain can be so severe that even a strong person can give up. That's why medical science says that people who are terminally ill should have loved ones around them. This is because their chances of survival are much higher when they are reminded that they have a reason to be alive.

Stephen had no reason to remain. In fact, he had more cause to leave than to stay because he saw something way better than where he was. On the other hand, Paul was stoned but just stood up as if they had just thrown feathers at him. The next day, after the disciples gathered around him, he departed. He wasn't carried on a stretcher; he departed to go to another city with Barnabas to preach.

Paul was passionate about his vision, which he mentioned in Philippians 1. I am not talking about a vision board; anyone can put anything on paper, even though it's not in their heart. We're discussing a vision that you've accepted as the reason why you are alive, a vision that you can die for. We don't have too many of those types of people today. A vision that you can sell all your belongings for. That kind of vision will keep you alive even though the devil wants to kill you.

ELIJAH

Elijah wanted to die when he went up the mountain to meet God. What did God do? God gave him a vision, something to live for. He told him to go and anoint Elisha. So anointing his successor and the two kings became his next vision, and he was taken to heaven when that was achieved. Your vision is tied to your purpose. It's best to have a vision that always keeps giving, a vision that you can never outgrow.

The Lord said to me many years ago that an ideology can never die. That's why you can keep killing the leader of Al Qaeda, ISIS, and they will just keep replacing them. These people are ready to die because they believe in their cause. It's a vision similar to Communism and Capitalism. When we give our lives to Christ, we don't give it so our spirits can live forever. Every human's spirit will live forever, but you're either living in Christ, eternal life, or in punishment, eternal damnation in hell. As long as the spirit has been birthed, it never dies. That's the same thing with the vision. The most dangerous people on earth believe in something they're ready to die for.

Accumulating money is not a good vision because you'll never have enough of it. A vision to have a 5000 ft² house is not a good vision. You want a vision that is a gift that keeps on giving. We want a vision you cannot achieve 100% on your own, a vision so big that you can pass it down to people coming after you. I heard a story of this great man of God, Archbishop Idahosa. At the age of about 60, he went around the world preaching over five times. Some people say he had preached to more black and white men than anyone alive. After touring Europe, he went back home to Nigeria. He sat down on his couch. He had been telling his wife that he felt as though he had completed all God told him to do. His wife tried to convince him that it was a sign of needing rest. He just kept saying that he had done everything God had told him to do. One day after a series of events at home, he sat down and was gone.

THE POWER OF FOCUS

Many of us are too distracted. If you look at the sun, the heat from the sun cannot burn anything on its own, but when you use a magnifying lens, suddenly, that heat is channeled, and with that, you can burn a piece of paper. That illustrates the power of focus. It takes effort to remain focused, but I assure you that the result will make the effort worthwhile. The moment you know your purpose, mission, and vision, decision-making becomes easy. Your purpose remains the same, but the vision will keep on changing. Once you have these three components, what you should study in school and the friends you should associate with will become very clear, and many of the questions we ask God will no longer be relevant.

A Pastor friend came to me a few years ago and said, "Since we are both Pastors and work in IT, being aware of the challenges churches have in this area, we should form a company together." I already knew that my answer was going to be no. Why? Because of my vision. That's not something I need to dabble in. I don't have time for that type of commitment. The extra time I have now is to drill deeper into what I know I have been called to do. Start running once you have located your vision from the beginning of the journey. Life is a race, and some people have not even started running yet.

My career mentor told a story about his first daughter. They were trying to force her to play soccer, but he said something happened that made them change their minds. One day, they were playing soccer on the field when she suddenly saw a flower. She stopped playing in the middle of the game to focus her attention on the flower. They said at that point, "We decided soccer was not best for her."

Some people are on the sidelines, while others are playing and scoring goals on the field. It is not because one person is dumb and others are smarter, but to a large extent, because of focus. This is why I thank God for this awesome privilege that we have in God through the Holy Spirit. Through proper guidance, a person can know that a particular direction is not the direction they need to go, and then suddenly, the one that people considered to be dumb is now shining, not because they've changed, but because the direction they're now going has changed.

STEPS TO ACTUALIZING A VISION

In essence, we want to answer the question, "Once God gives us the vision, what do we do next?" There are four main steps to take to run with your vision properly:

1. **Initial Stealth Mode**
2. **Share it With the Right People.**
3. **Put God First.**
4. **Watch, Run, and Pray.**

INITIAL STEALTH MODE

The first step is to stay in secret mode. You're not supposed to announce the vision to the whole world yet. It shouldn't be a post on Facebook or Instagram. When a woman is initially pregnant, it doesn't show yet until specific points in the process, and then the world begins to see. It is way more susceptible at the beginning stage, in the first trimester. Many visions are being aborted because they are shared prematurely. A wise person said that the light of a candle can easily be snuffed out, so use your palm to protect it when the wind is blowing. But the same wind that can put out a light in a candle can spread a wildfire. There is a point where your vision is just a flicker of light. Any little opposition can snuff it out, especially from loved ones. Not because they're wicked but because they love you. That's why they have to take the first shot at killing the vision. If you want to run with a vision, the book of Nehemiah is a good book to study because you'll see the beginning phase of the vision and how it was executed from beginning to end.

One of the best ways to protect yourself in initial stealth mode is by keeping quiet. In the case of Joseph, if he hadn't told his brothers about his dreams, they wouldn't have known. The Bible says that even a fool is considered wise if he keeps quiet. Another way is through prayer, putting God first in your decision-making processes, including the name of your business. Every Sunday, I see a vision or picture of what I am to wear. Is God interested in what I wear? Absolutely. You can involve God in as many things as possible.

You are deceiving yourself if you think you have received the vision because you've heard it. It takes a while. It might take years, months, weeks, or even days for some people. Let's hear from Paul, the Apostle. Galatians 1:16-17. When Paul initially got the revelation of who he was and his mission, he did not immediately go to the apostles or his friends. No. He left on a retreat and went to Arabia. Bible scholars say he was there for a few years and did not immediately show it.

There are some questions that people can ask you at that moment. If you cannot answer, it can affect your confidence. All you're supposed to do is just keep meditating on what God said. Let it be implanted in your heart. I pray that if you have ever aborted a vision, God restores it back to you in the mighty name of Jesus.

Revelations About Your Vision to Run With

When you receive revelations about your vision, how do you identify which one you're supposed to run with? God is not the author of confusion. He will confirm it, whether it is through people or from God. The meditation state is where you separate the wheat from the chaff. The Bible says that the truth is confirmed in the mouth of two or three witnesses. When you first get a vision, it is possible that even though you believe it was from God, it may actually have been from the devil; hence, a need to confirm. There are four voices we are able to hear:

1. **The Voice of God**
2. **People's Voices and Their Ideas**
3. **Your Own Voice Because You Have Your Own Mind**
4. **The Devil**

Any dream or vision can come from any of these four sources, no matter how vivid it is. This point may hit home for those with the prophetic gift. Just by being in proximity to someone, you can pick up what they are feeling or thinking. It's just like using an antenna if you have a prophetic gift.

Something happened in a previous ministry during one Sunday service. There were other churches in that building. We were having a service, and suddenly there was interference, and we began to hear what the church downstairs was saying in our own speakers. This is similar to times past when you would pick up your landline and start talking to someone, and suddenly your phone would pick up a frequency from someone else and then suddenly you'll have four people on the same phone line! It's possible to pick up what others are sensing or thinking.

It is elementary to think that because you had a dream and it was clear, then it must have been from God. Any of those four voices can be speaking to us, so it is critical that we meditate on those things in the initial stealth mode. We pray with them and ask if it is the Lord speaking to us. In the mouth of two or three witnesses, the truth is confirmed. God can send someone to confirm or debunk what you thought was from Him. That is how things are clarified. Some things can only be clarified with time, and you cannot rush. No matter what you do, the time has to go by because time is part of that process. Sometimes we are in such a hurry, but time is part of the process. The Bible says in Ecclesiastes 3:12 that, *"He has made everything beautiful in its time,"* including revelation and understanding. You do not share with friends or anybody; you keep meditating. You must learn how to incubate things deeply until they are implanted, and nothing can shake it.

Ways a Vision Can Be Killed at This Stage

1. **Through Loved Ones:** Our loved ones can be very inquisitive, asking a million questions because they do not want you to suffer losses. So you must be careful not to tell them about the vision too early. When did Jesus begin to tell His disciples that He was going to die? Toward the end of His ministry. Even then, Peter was against it and pulled Him to the side to rebuke Him. So if you do not have the self-control to keep things to yourself, you have to ask God for grace. This includes your spouse as well as anybody outside of yourself. Depending on the grace you have already built up in God, you can be in this state for a day. One can be in this state for a week, months, or years, depending on the heaviness of the spirit of rationalization, because it takes them a long time to believe anything. While some people are able to believe things quickly.

2. **Through Evil or Wicked People:** Some people want to snatch the vision from you. The effect, whether they love you or hate you, knowingly or unknowingly, is still the same. The vision can be lost.

When to Come Out of Initial Stealth Mode

How do you know you are ready to move to the next level? When no matter what anybody says or does not say, your vision is intact. Then you are ready to move forward.

I remember when I got the call into ministry. I shared the vision with the person above me in ministry, and they told me they didn't see the Pastoral grace in me. If I had shared that vision with him prematurely, that comment would have been the end of the pursuit of that vision. Even though it was already solid in me, I left that meeting almost shaken and had to go to God to ask Him to give me the Pastoral anointing and grace.

My parents knew me to be a very shy kid growing up. I could not even talk in front of my family members during family meetings. When I told them I would be a Pastor, my mom started laughing over the phone. You want to get to the point where regardless of the support you do or do not receive, you still move forward and are not shaken. The Bible says that the devil sometimes masquerades as an angel of light. The enemy has been here for a long time, and the Bible says the heart of man is very deep. We have been pushing some things for a long time that might mistakenly come back to the surface as a vision from God.

SHARE IT WITH THE RIGHT PEOPLE

The next step is to share the vision with the right team. However, many people make the mistake of sharing it on social media, which I see happening too often. All they do is register their business, and now the whole world knows about it without producing or gathering anything of substance. Anyone can register a business, so that is not the mark of success. Therefore, it's important to share the vision with the right team, which should consist of three categories of people.

Those Above You

The first category is those above you, such as mentors and spiritual authorities. You should share with them for clarification and validation, as your future is very important and should not be gambled away. If you only live once, then you should make your efforts count. For instance, when Paul returned from Arabia and Damascus, he spoke with the apostles about what God had said to him, and they validated it as being from God. This is similar to what happened in Nehemiah 2:17-18 and Matthew 4:18-22.

I don't know how many people's destinies have been messed up just because someone had a vision and saw themselves with a microphone but woke up and decided that God was calling them to be a Pastor when maybe God was saying that they could have been a conference speaker, motivational speaker, or CEO speaking to their staff. So, someone who was meant to be a business mogul could be stuck, suffering in ministry. This is where clarification is very important. The sad thing is that by the time people get to this point, they've gone so deep into their idea of the vision that it's very hard to get them out of it. It's almost like pulling teeth. Before getting too attached, you should share with those you have vetted.

If you share it with a true and proper authority before its time, it could still be protected, but there is a risk involved. Let me give you an example: when we go through marriage counseling, I tell people that they should not make their biological parents one of their mentors in marriage, no matter how anointed their parents are. They will always take a side if there is a challenge, and the person can never be at fault.

In another ministry, there was a situation where a couple had issues, and the man cheated on his wife. The man's sibling focused on what she must have done to cause him to cheat. In her eyes, her brother could do no wrong. She suggested that maybe the wife wasn't taking care of him properly. This is often what happens with loved ones. Therefore, those above you in the initial stealth mode do not necessarily mean parents. It refers to those in your holies of holies. Those above you to whom you have given access in that way should know.

From what we read in the book of Nehemiah, one of the decisions I made before coming into ministry was to speak the truth and nothing but the truth, regardless of anyone's feelings or what might not seem common or popular. And that is no different from what I am saying here. I have seen many people's destinies being aborted by parents and family members because they did not agree with it or didn't align with what they wanted for the person. At the end of the day, you will stand before God to give an account. Am I saying we should be rude? No, you should be tactful. The ultimate responsibility lies with each individual. I'll repeat it here: share the vision with those above you to clarify.

What happens in those odd cases where God says something clearly, but you go to authorities, and what they're saying is different from what God said, but you know you truly heard from God? If that person is truly your authority, then you need to go back to God to clarify. Why? There is a possibility that you both might have heard wrong. But you don't want to take that chance to just discard what they said that quickly. If they are truly an authority over you and have been vetted, it means that there is a track record of their opinions and counsel being valid.

I had to deal with a situation like that where I was mentoring someone in ministry, and they started to go in a different direction. They came to share their plans with me, and I said that it was not what they said God told them in the beginning. It was a very significant shift. I told them there was no way in good conscience that I could continue mentoring them. It was a fundamental thing. But in my heart, I still felt responsible for that person. Every now and then, they would come to my mind, I would feel compassion and pray for them.

After close to 5 years, the person realized they had gone in the wrong direction. They were restored, but what about the five years they had lost? We realized that certain voices had come into the mix when we examined what went wrong. They went in that direction because they started getting some results and assumed it was the right way to go. That's why results don't validate whether a direction is true or not. If a person is a true authority, don't be quick to discard what they say.

Your Colleagues

Once it has been clarified with those above you, you can share a bit of it with colleagues. Iron sharpens iron. The only people who should hear the details of your vision are those above you. Jealousy and envy are very dangerous virtues that can lead to people being killed or attacked in ways you cannot imagine. You will never know someone around you is jealous until there is an indication that something you're doing might end up making you more glorious than they currently are. Suddenly, you'll begin to see them in their true light at that point.

That is what happened to Joseph. He faced attacks when he told everybody that they were all bowing down to him. You had better be strong enough to defend yourself, especially if you lack self-control in that way. There are things that must be kept inside. The Bible says that when they told Mary about her son Jesus, she kept these things in her heart and didn't go around telling everyone. If you keep running your mouth, you should not be surprised when attacks start to come from everywhere. Why wouldn't they come? Jehu was very smart. When the prophet came to anoint him, he called him inside, and they anointed him. After Jehu was anointed, he went back to meet the other commanders and just sat down. They asked him what the prophet had said, and he downplayed it. He told them that the prophet said he was the king but that he didn't believe it.

Even though the people around you are not envious people, it is best not to tempt them. Your friend is not a thief, but why put a million dollars in front of them on the table and leave them in your house? Share the vision in phases with the people who will come together and work with you on the vision.

If you have already made the mistake of sharing everything with everybody, I will tell you a secret. In the movie "Men in Black," they used an apparatus to erase people's memories. God has the power to make people forget things. So if I say something people don't need to hear, I pray that the Lord will take those things out of their minds. How many times have you had vivid dreams but woken up with no idea what the dream was about? It's possible for people to lose the things they have. Don't engage with people. People are usually self-absorbed, so with enough time, they forget about it and focus on themselves if you don't engage in that conversation. Regardless of how openly it was shared, many people heard the prophecy of Jesus Christ coming, but Mary didn't go around talking to people.

How to Select the Right Team of People

Not just anybody can walk alongside you to fulfill a vision. If you look at Moses and Aaron, the only reason Aaron worked alongside Moses is that Moses forced God to bring Aaron along. Aaron almost crippled Moses' ministry. I've watched how people with a vision quickly bring their family and friends into it. In many cases, it's better for you if your family is out of it. There was a restaurant I used to go to. The food was nice, but when I would go there, I would see the kids of the owner running around and talking to guests. I would see friends and family just going in and out of the kitchen. I said to myself that this business would not last. And then it happened that they went out of business.

I actually saw a vision when I went to that place; I saw the restaurant going all over the globe. I even shared the vision with the owner, and he praised the Lord. The way everything was set up, the business was doomed to fail, even though God's desire was for it to prosper. Again, let's not judge them because some of us are going down the path where everything we do is done, trying to force family and friends to be a part of it. So how do you select the right team of people?

Through Prayer

The Bible said Jesus spent the whole night praying before He chose His disciples, yet there was still one Judas among them. That was God's plan. The fact that someone is offering their services does not mean it has to be accepted. Don't learn the hard way. The best way to know people is through prayer.

Prayer is also the best way to know who they will become. A situation happened in the United States where a man leading a ministry killed his wife. He shot her several times. Do you think she saw him as a killer when she married him? He must have been a lovely guy who opened the door for her, and one day he became a monster, but he had always been one. The best way to know people is through prayer. Some people don't even know what they themselves are capable of doing.

There is a man called Hazael who eventually became the king of Syria. When Elijah said that he would be the next king, even though he was a servant, the prophet was just looking at him and shaking his head. At some point, Hazael asked Elijah why he was looking at him like that. He was appalled at how destructive Hazael would be to the children of Israel, and Elijah told him of how he would tear pregnant women's bellies open. After hearing this, Hazael was shocked to hear that someone would say he would do such a thing. After he became king, however, he did much worse than that to the people. It was already seen way ahead of time. Through prayer, you can locate what a person can become, all things being equal.

Select People Who Walk With God

If it is a business, for example, it is important that your business partners are people who walk with God. You can work with non-believers, but your partners and those you share ownership with must have a close relationship with God. An employee does not own the business unless you give them shares, but if your partner is evil and not born again, what you have is also part of what can be attacked when judgment comes. That's what happened with Jehoshaphat. He got into certain dealings with an unbelieving king, and when God struck, he also suffered losses because what he had was connected to the evil king. It's like investing in a Ponzi scheme, and once it's exposed that your money is there, you can't say that your money was clean. It's part of it, and it goes down with everything else. Employees can be anybody.

For example, if you're a leader or a worker at Cornerstone Christian Church of God, you cannot say that you're not born-again. However, your accountant, banker, or whoever is filing the taxes does not have to be a born-again Christian. The church leadership has to be aligned; they have to be born-again Christians. That's the difference. You have your colleagues to keep you accountable and those under you who will assist you in doing the work because you can't run with a vision alone. They are also there to help lift and bear the burden, like in the case of Moses.

PUT GOD FIRST

Many people start well, but they don't end well because, down the line, they lose focus. Proverbs 16:3 and Matthew 6:33 instructs us to associate our business with God. Have you come across any Chinese restaurant that does not have the statue of Buddha in there? I haven't. It's us Christians who want to separate things. I am not telling you to find a picture of who they say Jesus looks like and post it on your business website. Just don't be afraid of the connection. Jesus said if you deny him before men, He will deny you before His Father. It doesn't have to be included in the name of the business, but let it be known and obvious.

You see some arguments that have arisen from non-Christian artists, and you hear some gospel songs where you can't even hear the name Jesus anywhere in the words. It's very scary. Don't deceive yourself. You're not trying to impress people. God should know that He is involved in your business, whether in how you choose your topics, the methodology used to validate your topics or the concepts with which you share ideas. Is it based on the Word of God or something else? In some form, your business has to be connected with God. When some Christians succeed, it will shock you how they start to get their ideas. Random people bring up ideas. When they started, they went to God to clarify things, but now that they're successful, they feel like they can decide what they want to do for themselves. You can put God first in the vision. You can put God first financially. When Abraham went to conquer to retrieve Lot and his people, he gave God a tithe of all. This is proof that God was involved in Abraham's business financially.

Involve God in Your Hiring Process

One of the leaders at CCCG was a manager overseeing about 37 people. She told me that after they had a legal case where one of the staff misbehaved and accused a church member of impropriety, she admitted that this was the only person she hadn't prayed about before she hired. Everyone else she had prayed about, but not that specific person. "The just shall live by faith and not by sight."

WATCH, RUN, AND PRAY

Finally, you need to watch, run, and pray when running with a vision. This category is put this way because when you are running with the vision and begin to succeed, opposition will come. If opposition does not come, either:

1. **You're Sleeping and Oblivious to it. It's There and You've Been Captured Already.**
2. **Somebody Else is Fighting the Battles for You.**

When you are succeeding, there will be opposition. Never allow your vision to take you away from God. It's very easy to be doing God's work without God; to keep doing what is right, but God is not in it anymore. Be sensitive, run, and pray. In the course of moving with the vision, you can suffer burnout, so you need to adjust yourself. Watch your associations and the kinds of people you surround yourself with. Unless you're looking ahead, you can never be inspired. I read biographies of the people ahead of me in ministry because their stories inspire me to keep moving forward.

The spirit of slumber operates more frequently when you are around people who are not your equals. Who you surround yourself with and who you share your vision with matters. We know the start of a vision, but we don't know its end. When we die to go be with the Lord, the vision He gave us must never die; it must always continue. Derek Prince, for example, has gone to be with the Lord, but they are still releasing videos almost every week. Steve Jobs is gone, but Apple is a trillion-dollar business today.

A time will come when aspects of your vision will be public knowledge. However, specific plans will not be public knowledge to anyone, and you won't share that with others. So, let's say Facebook wants to go into electric vehicles in ten years; nobody should know that until they're ready to implement it.

The previous examples are different ways you can compartmentalize the implementation of your vision. These things take some work, but we're up to the task by the grace of God. Put your head to the ground, stay focused, mind your own business, and focus on what God has called you to do. In no time, you'll begin to see the vision begin to blossom. Success has many friends, and many people will begin to come. Apply principles. It's not any Tom, Dick, or Harry that you should bring in just because they desire to be involved in the vision. And you'll see that if you put the proper boundaries in place, everything will flourish by the grace of God.

Once you've captured a vision, it will become very obvious that you've caught it. The kind of friends you move with will be determined by the vision you've caught, and how you schedule your life will also reflect that vision. Let your life demonstrate that you've truly caught the vision, and eventually, we'll see it. When the vision is documented, it's called a plan. Many of us write these things down, and we have a plan. Having a vision without steps is like building castles in the air.

There's a saying that goes, "If wishes were horses, even beggars would ride." But when a plan is attached to the wish, you suddenly mean business. The moment we capture a vision, it becomes very obvious, just like someone offering me a job and asking me to work on Sunday - I don't need to go to God in prayer because it directly clashes with what I've been called to do. You don't need to announce that you have a vision; let your life demonstrate that you've truly caught it, and we'll eventually see it.

Allow the Holy Spirit or human authorities to validate what you're capable of doing, not yourself, because you'll either push yourself to the point of exhaustion or you won't push yourself to the capacity the Holy Spirit expects of you. When I hear an authority sharing testimonies about what they do and how to navigate things, and I look at myself and realize I'm still scratching the surface, it pushes me to know that operating at the top level is possible.

Some people allow their body, mind, or emotions to tell them what they're capable of doing. If you know where you're going, the next logical question is, "What do I need to get there?" In some cases, you would need to end some relationships in order to actualize your vision. The moment a person sees that they can't manage a friendship because friendships require attention, then they have too many friends. They can't keep up anymore because they can't service those friendships accordingly. There are different levels of friendships. Some are acquaintances, some are best friends, whatever you want to call them.

In my mind, when you stop being able to handle and carry that many relationships, that's when you potentially need to drop some things because they have expectations of you that you cannot meet. Personally, I don't have too many friends because it's a lot of work, but the ones I do have, we run very deep. I don't have friendships I have to maintain daily because I don't have the time. I always say that fulfilling your purpose is crucial. You must do what it takes to make sure your vision is not lost.

8

Leading With Love (Part 1)

A leader is like a platform on which people stand. The people being led are the ones standing on the platform. Someone once said that if they see further, it's because they're standing on the shoulders of giants. That's what leadership is all about. John Maxwell would say that leadership without succession is not leadership. This means that succession should be one of the primary motives of leadership. What do I mean by succession? Leading people who can do better than you and be better than you. What do I mean by leading with love? Psalm 25:10. Let's start with loving God. You cannot effectively lead people without loving God. God is the source of love. No human being has love in themselves to give. What we have is lust.

The difference between love and lust is that one is selfless, and the other is selfish. Love motivates a person to take steps without necessarily focusing on what they will get back in return, but lust is selfish. A person who lusts can take the same steps as a person who loves, but the motive for the person lusting is personal fulfillment and satisfaction.

Let's use a man and a woman as an example. A man can pursue a woman because he thinks he loves her and starts doing all kinds of things, buying gifts, opening doors, and making wonderful gestures. In reality, he might only be doing these things because he is physically attracted to her and wants to sleep with her. Another man, on the other hand, might do the same things because he actually loves her. The actions are the same, but the goal of one is destruction and personal satisfaction, and the goal of the other is to express real love.

We saw this in one of David's sons. The Bible used the word love, but it should have been lust. David's son, Amnon, claimed to love his sister, but in reality, he lusted after her. His obsessive lust eventually led him to rape her, and immediately he did, he despised and chased her away from his presence. That was not love. The so-called love was no more when he got what he strongly desired.

LOVE FOR GOD

Leading with love starts with loving God. When you love God, you will love the House of God and the kingdom of God. What is the kingdom of God? The kingdom of God is the entire body of Christ. It's not one church. You would love everything that glorifies Jesus. And because we love His kingdom, we give our resources to the advancement of His work. As a church, we give to other Ministries. When we were doing the renovations, I asked God where to get the money from. He told me to sow a seed into another ministry that was undergoing its own renovations. That instruction didn't make sense at the time, but I obeyed.

We cannot lead if we do not love; we get love from God because God is love. You know the light bulb is not the source of electricity; it is just channelled so that we can connect to where it is being generated. Our job is to plug into God and receive enough love to give. When people say they are tired of being nice, that's a person who is starved of love.

We demonstrate our love for God because we love His kingdom. I see Christians today, especially on social media, destroying the kingdom. When you join people who attack ministers, you are attacking the body of Christ. You're giving unbelievers the right to do these things. Why not pray for them instead of attacking people and airing their shortcomings? Do you know how many Pastors commit suicide in a year? Many, especially in North America, but the ones that make the news are the 'popular preachers.'

The Bible says that some women ministered to Jesus with their substance. Do you know who those women were? About eight women. How many disciples did Jesus have? Multitudes. At some point, he had

70, at another point, he had one hundred twenty, according to the Bible. He was preaching to multitudes. If you keep saying somebody else will do it, then nobody does it. People who choose to serve the kingdom choose to forgo specific things just so they can be at service to the kingdom of God. Jesus went to the home of Lazarus, Mary, and Martha for a reason. Many people were more focused on what they could get from Jesus, but Mary, Martha, and Lazarus were different; they saw Him as the Messiah but also as a human being, and He was comfortable in their home.

DISPLAYING THE LOVE OF GOD

Desire to See the Kingdom of God Advance

If you read the account of Luke, the Bible talks about Simeon and Anna, the prophetess. Anna was widowed at a young age but stayed in the temple, serving God day and night in fasting and prayer. What was she fasting and praying about? That the Messiah should come. So her focus was on the kingdom of God.

For those kinds of people, God answers their prayers without them even asking. Do you pray for the kingdom of God? I don't even know if I pray for myself at all. Only God knows. Are you the Pastor? No, but you love the kingdom of God. As mentioned in a previous example, someone had a vision of me preaching: From the audience, she saw a whole bunch of arrows coming. Since that point, she realized that preaching is special warfare; it's not motivational speaking.

I heard of a particular person who came to a place for ministry work. He felt something happen while he was preaching, and then his mouth began to swell up. It was sudden. Arrows were flying. Not everybody who comes to church in person or online is here for God. Some are witches sent by the devil. Some may not realize but some do.

Jesus cast out seven demons from Mary, so I love everyone and want to see them all transformed, perfected, and strengthened if they allow God to touch them.

Do you know how many Pastors are being set up on a daily basis? One time a lady went to the ministry for help but took her child and hid her child outside of the church. She pretended she had brought her child with her and claimed that the Pastor had taken the child. By the time the police got involved and investigated, they realized she had put her child somewhere. There were security cameras. They were literally watching her put her daughter in a specific place. What is the motive behind these things? It is the devil. That's why prayer is so important: "Lord, keep your church, strengthen your church, and empower your church."

Love What God Loves

The Bible says, *"For God so loved the world that He gave His only begotten Son..."* (John 3:16) We have pre-service prayers before Sunday service that are targeted toward praying for the ministry, the ministers, and the people. Paul said if you love me, pray for me. So if you love God, you will pray for your Pastor. Some people don't understand what will happen to them if they lose their Pastor or if something happens to the Pastor.

DEEPENING YOUR LOVE FOR GOD

We know that God already loves us, so how do we plug into that power so that we can be powered ourselves in love?

Obedience

You will feel the love of God so much every time you obey God. I learned this through practice, and it is also scriptural. You will feel approved, accepted, fathered, loved, and covered by God. Jesus said, "If you love me, keep my commandments."(1 John 5:1-3) So we obey his written commandments and his revealed commandments. If commandments are too old-school for you, then just say instructions. If the word instruction is too hard to accept, just say His strong recommendations. Whatever works for you. I take them as instructions. I don't have a choice. Once he says it, I have to do it whether I like it or not. So if you feel like God doesn't love you, look for any of his instructions and obey them, and you'll feel the love come so strongly. *"For as many as are led by the Spirit of God, these are sons of God."* (Romans 8:4)

Can you point to something God told you to do that you actually did? I'm not saying when you were hungry, God told you that you should eat. I'm not talking about that! I am talking about things you did not want to do, but the only reason you did those things is because God told you to do them. We need to move beyond the level of baby Christianity, where it's only the instructions we like that we do, but the moment God touches on the things we don't like, we begin to throw a tantrum like a child.

For people who genuinely walk with God, most of the things they obey cannot be openly broadcasted. Paul said, *"I know a man in Christ who fourteen years ago—whether in the body I do not know, or whether out of the body I do not know, God knows—such a one was caught up to the third heaven. And I know such a man—whether in the body or out of the body I do not know, God knows— how he was caught up into Paradise and heard inexpressible words, which it is not lawful for a man to utter."* (2 Corinthians 12:2-4) Not every revelation or vision is to be publicly shared.

While God forgives, there are levels where God's forgiveness will be delayed. Moses begged God not to kill the Israelites, and even though God forgave them, Moses hit the rock instead of speaking to it as God instructed, and God said he would never enter the promised land. When Moses brought it up, God told him never to bring it up again. To whom much is given, much is expected. Moses and Christ are people who saw the face of God, and God expected more from Moses. This principle is closely connected to honour. Therefore, if you're not able to love and honour those you can see, your fellow brothers and sisters, it's impossible to love God, whom you cannot see. We know we love God by obeying his instructions in the Bible, which he spoke to us in our private time. Some people were told by God not to marry specific people, but they still did, and they claimed to love God.

Walking in Forgiveness

1 Peter 4:8 and Matthew 5:43-48. In an average church, family, group of people, or even Christians, it's easy to find many people holding onto offence against someone else. One way to know God is moving through a person is when they decide to let the past go. Some people still need space because they are crazy and haven't changed. You may still forgive them, but they're still dangerous.

To be honest, it's not easy to forgive. You'll find the energy to do it when you've just spent time with God. Everyone makes mistakes, but it gets more difficult when people are not asking for forgiveness. Our job is still to give it regardless. I heard a quote about forgiveness that I will never forget, which may have been attributed to Nelson Mandela. People asked him how he felt about being in prison for 27 years. People were surprised when he was finally released and started working together with those who imprisoned him. He said that refusing to forgive is like drinking poison and expecting someone else to die.

When you hold onto offence, you are killing yourself, but in your mind, you feel like holding on will hurt the other person. Unforgiveness dries a person up, while forgiveness releases the individual. Matthew 18 gives an example of this point taught by Christ. The Bible recounts a story of a king who forgave the unforgiving servant, but then the servant turned around and demanded his right from the one who owed him money and locked him up in prison. People heard and were not pleased, and they told the king. The king took that man and his whole family and locked them up. One reason why it is relatively easy for me to let go of things is that I remember where I came from and how much God has forgiven me.

You can be close to God and think you're good, but have you always been good? There is a judgmental nature among Christians who forget where they came from and look down on people who just came to Christ, expecting them to develop wings and begin to fly. They make one mistake, and they judge them, asking how they could make that mistake. Focus on your relationship with God. My parents are Pastors, and I should have been a superstar Christian from birth! I should have been casting out demons from the moment I was crawling! But I did crazy things. I am glad I am still alive; God is very faithful.

When I was much younger and in school, I did bad things, and whenever I got back home, I became a Christian again. However, God arrested me in Poland and said I would die if I didn't serve Him. I had all kinds of supernatural manifestations and finally gave my life to Christ. And it's been amazing ever since.

Giving to God

John 3:16 shows that every time there is love, there is giving. The only thing that comes to people's minds when people talk about giving is money because that is something valuable to people. So let's say you're in a relationship with someone, and you can't remember what he or she has given to you. At that point, there is a problem. You're not a gold digger, but it is still your right. You're not dependent on that person financially, but on the other hand, there are expectations. Their birthday, Valentine's, and Christmas went by, but still no gift.

You went shopping for yourself and didn't even think of your significant other.

In the same vein, giving money is part of your display of love to God. I find it hard to believe when someone says they love God and don't give to Him financially. It's like living in your parent's home as a grown-up and working but not contributing to anything in the house like utilities or food and saying that you love your parents and siblings. If you love God, it must show in your finances. In our own home, our greatest expense is towards God, next is our investments. We need to adjust our priorities to ensure we put our money where we claim our heart is.

Giving to God also includes giving him our attention. The way our car runs on gas should be the way we run on God. In every aspect of our lives, He should be involved. In the beginning, it would seem like you're losing control, but that's because we are used to being in control.

When I was a Youth Pastor, I was working a full-time job, but I was stressed. You could see my eye bags. I remember one day, I was sitting in the church office in preparation, so numb and aloof, just staring into nothing. The head Pastor came and looked at me and asked if I was okay. What was I doing? It's because I was doing everything myself. The moment I handed it over to God, I started doing exponentially more than I did back then. I've decided to give him my best every day. He who stands should take heed lest he falls. Every day, I give Him my best in the areas of time, decision-making, and everything.

I want to speak specifically to a group of people who have more than two jobs. I would like you to ask yourself a critical question: Why? What are you pursuing? I can most likely tell you that your relationship with God is not growing at the pace it ought to grow. To build a relationship, you need time. The weight is not on the fact you're doing more than one job but on the responsibilities you have signed up to take.

On an accounting level, many people don't know that the moment you cross a specific point of income, it becomes less profitable. There's a difference when all that you are doing is going in the direction of your calling. For many people with multiple jobs, it's not about the calling; it's about the money. Did God tell you to do it? Of course, if God told you to apply for six jobs, you should take the necessary steps to do it. If someone gives you a job offer, you should be able to tell them that you need a little bit of time. Take this time to bring your questions and confirm with God. In some cases, He will confirm with you at the actual interview. But if someone is telling you that you have to make an immediate decision, that is suspicious because you should be able to take the time to think about what is being offered and show them that you are not desperate.

EVIDENCE YOU HAVE YIELDED TO GOD

There are two aspects to consider:

1. **Giving Your Worries to God**
2. **Receiving Rest From Him**

When I started my Ph.D., I asked God how to fit it into my schedule, and He told me to find two hours every weekday and four hours every Saturday and that I would be just fine. So I gave it to God, and then He gave me a strategy to apply. Now, I could have given it to Him and not asked Him for help in strategizing. You know you have given it to God when you are at rest. Once it is on your plate, you are stressed out.

Are you worried about Canada's defence when it comes to other countries? No, you are at rest because you know that there is a Ministry of Defence to protect Canadian borders. Rest is evidence that you have handed it over to Him. Jesus said that His yoke is heavy and His burden is light. He said that all of you who labour and are heavy-laden, come to Him, and He will give you rest. Sometimes we have given things in prayer to God, but we are still carrying them because we are so used to carrying burdens.

LOVE FOR YOURSELF

The next aspect of leading with love is loving yourself. Being led by a leader with low self-esteem is dangerous, like Saul. Those types of leaders would want to bury the ones that they're leading the moment they see any indication that they are shining. Joshua ran to Moses and said that there was someone prophesying in the camp, and he told him to shut up because Moses was the only prophet who should be prophesying. Moses told Joshua that he actually wished that everyone in Israel would prophesy. Let them shine. That's why I am happy when I hear that God is touching people through other leaders, workers, and other members of the congregation.

God asked me before I started the ministry what kind of ministry I wanted. I didn't know because I didn't know what kind of ministries are out there. He asked if I wanted an Old or New Testament ministry. He said that an Old Testament ministry is like the ministry of Moses, who was the center of attraction and the one with the rod. In the New Testament ministry, the apostles did not have rods; they were performing miracles, but the deacons and the people were also doing miracles. God was moving through people as they were filled with the Holy Ghost.

That's why I love leadership classes, where people are mentored and imparted with the knowledge and skills to replicate the grace of their mentors. Wise leaders avoid people who try to praise them over their mentors. Some have said those things to me, but I just laugh them off because people are looking for my downfall, whether they know it or not.

Insecure leaders cannot love themselves, so they must learn to love themselves first by knowing that they are no longer who they used to be, as stated in 2 Corinthians 5:17. The foundation for loving ourselves the way God wants us to is knowing that the love of God must overshadow every other love, and we must love our neighbours as ourselves. From a practical perspective, this means that I know who I am in Christ, what God has enabled me to do, and what He has blessed others with. I can appreciate the gifts that God has given others without comparing them to mine. Therefore, when it's time for me to step into my area of expertise, I do so with boldness. When it comes to other things, I will try if people are not there. Once they arrive, I will step back so that they can take the stage.

Loving yourself begins with taking an inventory of who you are as a person. Let me ask you a question: do you know who you are? I often write out my strengths and areas for improvement so that I can take an inventory of who I am as a person. What am I good at? What are the things I am not good at? I would rather not focus on the things I am not good at. This allows me to have a balanced view of myself. Taking it from your head and putting it on paper is important. If you are naturally optimistic, all you have in your head are your strengths, so you tend to lean toward the side of pride. If you are naturally pessimistic, all you have in your head are your weaknesses, which can lead to low self-esteem. Putting it on paper will help show a balanced view of both. This way, you can see that you're good but need other people as well and that you're not that bad.

One of the reasons people don't love themselves is because they don't see themselves. In the United States of America, there was a social experiment where some women were told to describe their size after losing weight. Most of them exaggerated their current size, which meant that even though they had physically lost weight, in their mind, they still had the weight they had lost. So it's one thing to achieve certain successes, but it's another thing for it to register in your mind, and you recognize that you're no longer where you used to be. This gives us the right mental picture of who we are as people. If you saw yourself, would you love yourself?

BALANCING YOUR VIEW OF YOURSELF

How do we have a balanced view of ourselves? We can do that by answering a few questions.

Where Do I Belong?

The enemy will never allow some people to find the right church and stay there because it adds to a sense of security in who they are. Where is my place? Finding your place has a significant impact on you. That's the spot where your gifts are needed and who you are is appreciated. It makes you feel like you're in heaven.

How Much am I Worth?

As I began to grow in my understanding, it hit me one day that if someone invested money in me, they would never lose that investment. That is because I am confident in who I am. I know that I am not a liability but an asset. If I could buy you, what price tag would you put on yourself? Some people would say one trillion dollars. Is that really true? How much did it take for someone to get you to give up on the values that you hold dear to you? That's the real estimate of what you think you're worth on a practical level.

How Much am I Willing to Invest in Myself?

The amount of money you're willing to invest in yourself determines your true value or what you think you're worth. Some people can go to a store and spend $100 or $200 on a gift for someone else, but when they want to buy something for themselves, they would never spend that much. Even when it's the blackest Black Friday sales, they don't believe they deserve anything of value. I'm not saying that if you can't afford it, you should use your credit card to buy something for yourself. That's not smart.

There was a lady who would constantly buy me gifts, and I noticed that she would never buy anything for herself. So, I asked about it, and she said she was waiting for sales. I said, "No, no, no. That is not right, and it's not healthy love. Loving someone more than you love yourself? Go and buy something for yourself." One day, she reached out to me and said that she bought a $100 gown, and it was a major event for her!

How else will you know how much you're worth? When people bless you with things, what happens to you? Do you look at it and say, "No, how could you give this to me?" Or are you very grateful because you deserve those things? When you look at people blessing you with something, the way that you respond to it is an indication of your value. God knew that He could request Isaac from Abraham because He knew that He was worth it and deserved that kind of sacrifice because He is God.

What am I Able to Do?

This speaks to your capacity, capability, and gifts. One of the things I repeatedly heard from the messages I preached on 'The Five-fold Offices' was how edifying it was for people to know where they belonged: being an evangelist, a teacher, an apostle, a pastor, or a prophet. My point is to learn what you are able to do with ease or what you don't need preparation for. It boosts your confidence. What can you easily do even after you've just woken up from sleep?

I was having a conversation with someone many years ago, and she told me she was dumb. I told her that God doesn't create any dumb person and asked how she concluded that she was dumb. She said it was because she didn't know math and told me what her teachers would say. I told her she didn't have to know math to be brilliant. Math is just a subject. I began to ask questions, like what are the things that she loved to do. After our conversation, she lit up because she realized that there's no one way of measuring brilliance. This whole thing about IQ was put together for a specific reason. It's not a measure of intelligence by any means.

No exam can measure intelligence. Some people can look at a piece of art and explain everything; they are extremely artistic. Some people don't know they are incredibly gifted and talented because our educational system does not account for it. This is part of the reason why I am passionate about education. You see people who, just because of their experience growing up in schools, have concluded that they are dumb.

I was attending a lecture when I was part of a study group, and the man speaking was of Chinese descent. I could barely understand what he was saying because the English was fragmented. At some point, he paused and said, "You know, this is why it's good to succeed in life. I am a multimillionaire. Now it is your problem to understand me!" He said it was his problem to make sure other people understood when he first started, but now that he's rich, it's not his problem.

DISCOVER:
YOUR STRENGTHS & WEAKNESSES

As a leader, we can't make decisions for people. There's a difference between mentoring the people we lead and working with them. Some people want to improve, so they allow us to take them outside their comfort zone. Others are uninterested in that and want to remain in their comfort zone. They may not say it, but their actions show it, so we keep them in their comfort zone. If we don't know our strengths or weaknesses, we can speak with our Pastor, close relatives, or mature friends who can objectively tell us these things.

We should find a healthy space where those types of conversations can be had. I wouldn't really go the friend route because some people have different types of friends. A friend who can't tell you when you make a mistake is not a friend who should work through those types of things.

My wife shared her testimony that she thought she didn't have any skills when we first met. I laughed the first time because I thought she was joking, but I realized she wasn't laughing. Why? Her older sister is a skilled artist in the United Kingdom. She sings, acts, and does all kinds of things. Growing up, she was constantly compared to her sister. She almost learned to measure her capabilities based on her sister's. We began to explore, and today, if I allowed her, she could organize my whole life for me; that's a gift. No matter how much a person can sing, they need a manager.

You have a uniqueness that the world needs. From an Apostolic perspective, God has given me the gift to identify people's gifts, where they ought to be, and the steps they need to take to get there if they are willing to take those steps. That's why you see people at CCCG, to the glory of God, who have received restoration, no matter how short or long they have been here. All to the glory of God.

Minimize Your Focus on Weaknesses

What are you not able to do? As much as you can, avoid dwelling on those things. The more you do the things you're not good at, the more your confidence will take a hit. The Bible says that pride comes before a fall because when a person is proud, they don't objectively measure their weaknesses. They underestimate them, so the devil pushes them to do those things because he knows they will fail. The more they fail, the more their confidence is attacked.

Having the right mental picture is knowing where your areas of expertise are, the things that you're good at, and those you're not. You may ask a question about any weaknesses you may need to improve to move forward with your purpose. I can argue that question and thought. I am a first principles thinker, which means that I honour principles and systems, but I still keep in mind that there are potential things that may be unnecessary to attempt. What do I mean? Instead of accumulating or acquiring the experience or talent myself, I pay for someone with that specific experience or skill.

Do you know that there was a time when everybody baked their own bread before they had bakeries? Now, most people still can't bake their own bread. There was a time when the milkman used to bring milk every day, but now, we can't even remember that. Many things we think we need to know are no longer necessary; we can buy into other people's gifts and make them do the work for us.

I was listening to a Jewish Rabbi one time who was talking about Jewish secrets. One thing that the man said that stood out and is common in the Jewish community was that if their neighbour started a business, you would hardly find that family doing that service themselves. They would rather outsource the service to that person. That's why you see them growing. And you would hardly find a Jewish family that is not enterprising. It's a mindset.

What do I really need to know personally to succeed and excel? I was praying and fasting one day, and the Lord told me that I should never do anything that I am not the best at and that I must now look for other people who are the best at it. I must never do it myself. Immediately after that, I found somebody, got them to do it, and moved on. So it's good for you to know these principles so that as God expands you, you will know what to hold on to and what to let go of in life. That's what Jethro taught Moses in the wilderness, the art of delegation. If you focus more on improving your weaknesses than your strengths, your confidence will always be lower than it's supposed to be. Focusing on strengths allows us to build our confidence.

When I am mentoring people, the goal is not for them to get better at something they're not good at. The goal is to have them locate and become better in their area of strength. They can eventually tackle their weaknesses as they grow in their strengths and become more confident. But the weaknesses are not the focus. You find believers who are so sin-conscious. Every time they come to church, they are reminded that they are not good enough. Colossians 2:9-10. Am I saying that we are all perfect? No. But according to God's eyes, we are already perfect and are walking towards perfection daily.

Minimize Your Focus on Your Sins

Ask yourself a question. How much better have you become since you have been focusing on sin? It will just keep multiplying. I don't think about sin. I am the righteousness of God in Christ Jesus. I am already righteous, but I trust Him daily for grace to keep improving. If your heart does not condemn you before God, you are right before God. So I just keep doing my thing, and if there is no conviction, move forward.

Some people ask for forgiveness before every prayer, every single day. What kind of relationship is that? It seems like it's just in case they did something wrong. If a friend started every conversation with, "Just in case I did anything bad, forgive me," you would suspect they had done something wrong. That was the problem of the older brother of the prodigal son. He was just as messed up as the prodigal son. One left physically, but one had already left emotionally. The Bible chose to focus on the one who left physically, but the Bible is a book of instructions, doctrines, and directions. The Bible also states that the truth is confirmed in the mouth of two or three witnesses. This scenario is something to think about because the Bible is very practical.

Let's say you woke up at 6:00 a.m. this morning and prayed the Lord's Prayer, asking God for forgiveness. You asked Him to forgive you of your trespasses just in case you sinned while sleeping. Then, when you got to work and talked to God again, you asked for forgiveness because you might have sinned when you were coming from home to work. At 10:00 a.m., you prayed again, asking for forgiveness for your trespasses in case you sinned at work. When you got home, you prayed for forgiveness of your trespasses again, and the next morning you did the same thing. The Lord's Prayer is a model to follow, which means that these are the components of a healthy prayer life, not just a healthy prayer session.

If you study the prayers of the Apostles, like in Acts 4:31 when they were beaten, and they went back to their brethren and began to pray, you'll see that there were some things they didn't touch on, but their prayer was focused on God's Kingdom coming on earth as it is in heaven. The Bible says they were filled with boldness, the Holy Ghost came upon them, and the ground shook, so God answered that prayer. The point here is that Jesus gave us the Lord's Prayer as a model, and you won't find any other prayer in the New Testament that follows the Lord's Prayer.

There are times when the Holy Ghost convicts me, and because I know that asking for forgiveness is part of a healthy prayer life, I repent. Then I move on. The next time I talk to God in prayer, my heart is not condemning me, so I'm not asking God for forgiveness of anything. But if I'm convicted of sin, I repent and ask for forgiveness right then and there. It's a dynamic relationship with God.

9

Leading With Love (Part 2)

DETERMINING YOUR VALUE

Some people attribute their worth to how much material wealth they can accumulate, their relationship status, or their appearance. However, what we are supposed to attribute our worth to is what the Word of God says about us. I remember reading Psalm 139:14 many years ago, which said I am *"...fearfully and wonderfully made..."* That exploded within me. Fearfully and wonderfully made! You can hear that scripture, look in the mirror, and not see anything fearful, but you've missed it. What you see in the mirror can be changed. God was talking about the value He has put inside of us that nobody can change. That's what He said He made fearfully and wonderfully. I know people who used to have a six-pack, and now they have a one-pack or two-pack. Even your height and complexion can change.

When you ask someone about the value of a thing, one of the first things we see the value for is how much they bought it for. So what's the value in the open market? The value of a soul is Jesus. The Bible says, *"God so loved the world that he gave his only begotten Son."* (John 3:16) So Jesus came to die on the cross for you and for me. In fact, when Jesus died, we were not even born yet. So if there were only two human beings on earth, Jesus would have still come to die on the earth for those two people. Therefore, the value of every soul is the very life of Jesus, the Son of God. For me, that is extremely valuable.

To make sense of these things, we need to meditate on them. Unfortunately, many of us have saturated our minds with destructive comments we've heard from people, like "You're stupid, you're foolish." This is, therefore, the picture that has formed in the person's mind. Some of us have experienced abuse, so that's the picture that has formed. However, that is not how we determine value.

I've watched with amazement how God has transformed people's lives, which I have seen firsthand in CCCG. The apostles say that we can only say what our eyes have seen and what our hands have handled. I've seen how God transformed a person who felt like they weren't good enough and that all they wanted to do was kill themselves into someone who is now a sight to behold! You would never know if they didn't tell you that they almost killed themselves.

Someone shared with me that they took a lot of sleeping pills the night before just to commit suicide. I've said time and time again that if I don't release you, you will not die if you're truly under my authority. That person is now getting to know that they have value. What was the enemy trying to do? He convinced the person that they didn't have value and did not need to be alive. This is why this lesson and many others are very important. It all starts with the thought that you are not good enough. If you allow it and you don't fight it, the next day, the enemy will add something else to it until the suggestion of killing yourself comes.

When I see people allowing themselves to be in abusive relationships, I see someone who doesn't know their value. They think that is the best life can afford them. Someone shared with me that different men were saying that if she wanted to keep herself and not engage in premarital sex, no guy would be interested in her. What kind of boys, not men, was she talking to? I know reasonable men of God who have decided to be in a relationship without having sex until marriage. It all boils down to value. When you know your value, and someone comes up with a proposition that makes no sense, you can easily turn it down because you know your value.

HOW TO BE CONFIDENT IN YOUR VALUE

Meditating on the Word of God and our values. Some of us have been taught that meditating on our strengths is pride. Knowing your strengths is not pride. Knowing that you are good in certain areas is confidence. If you already love God and people, the missing link is loving yourself, and that is just what we need to increase so that everything balances properly. That's the whole basis behind Jesus' statement, *"I am the way, the truth, and the light."* Me saying I am a man is not pride but a fact. In the same way, you say that you are a gifted singer, if you are, is a fact, not pride. But when you say that you sing better than someone else, 'that' is pride.

All I am saying is to acknowledge the strengths that God has given to you. There is nothing wrong with knowing who you are and what you can do because sooner or later, the enemy will come knocking and try to tell you that you're not good enough. If you've already prepared for those things, you can reply and tell him to keep quiet. God didn't make you without any gifts. These are the things you can do well. There are times when you can compare yourself with other people, but it has to be within the parameters of achieving a purpose. Jesus corrected his disciples when they argued about who was the greatest. They were comparing. Jesus said that the one who will be the greatest is the one who is a servant.

Who is a servant? A servant is one who assumes a position of service knowingly. How can you serve someone if you don't have something to offer? He is saying that the way we can compare more is by asking ourselves how we can add value to someone's life. What area does this person need help in that I can support?

The Bible helps us take a long-term view of things. When you compare, initially, it can be fine, but the Bible says that there is a way that seems right unto a man, but its end is the way of death. God already sees the end from the beginning. It may look good now, but what happens when someone suddenly and drastically outperforms everybody else? Then envy begins to come as well. Remember, the Bible says that all kinds of evil come in. Murder began with Cain and Abel. It's one of the reasons why I love messages about the five offices, where each person identifies who they are so they know their lane and stay focused on it. In comparison, it's about how I can add value to other people better than they can themselves. That is the only extent of healthy comparison.

Let's read 1 Peter 1: 18-19. This passage validates what we are, who we are, and what we have loaded on the inside of us. God can restore anybody and anything if we only come to Him with an open mind. He is the Master Potter. We have inestimable value to the kingdom of God.

We have been equipped by the Holy Spirit to do the work that God has given us to do. One of the ways people feel a lack of confidence is in their ability. Their ability in school, a relationship, or different spheres can quickly weaken a person's confidence. The Bible tells us that we have the Holy Ghost on the inside of us that can make us able. Paul said in Philippians 4:13, "*I can do all things through Christ who strengthens me.*" He didn't say, 'I will do all things' because that is foolish; he said, 'I can' if I'm instructed to do so. We are not called to do all things. Jesus was not a doctor or going around to study law or randomly jumping from one occupation to another. Because I can do it, it doesn't mean I'm supposed to do all things.

OPERATING OUTSIDE OF YOUR GIFTING

I realized that one of the ways the devil has attacked people's confidence is by tempting them to take on things they are not gifted to do. The devil tempts you, saying, "If you are truly gifted, then why don't you go up there and sing like that person?" That is called temptation. You know deep down that God hasn't given you that gift, and when you sing, people run away.

I always wondered about the story of David and Goliath. The Bible said something interesting. In those days, the armies would gather to charge against each other. Something strange happened. The Israelites gathered on the mountaintop, and the Philistines gathered on the mountaintop as well, and the Bible said something interesting. The Bible said that Goliath would come down to the valley every morning and every evening and tell the Israelites to send one person to meet him in the valley to fight.

Whoever won would take the others as slaves. That was not how they used to fight battles then, but Goliath and the Philistines wanted to change the rules of engagement. When Goliath went down into the valley, the king could have said to the warriors, "Shoot all the arrows into the valley, and make sure that he did not come out alive because he put himself in a vulnerable situation." That is the power of temptation. If there is pride, you will easily fall.

In early America, they used to engage in dual matches where they would face and try to kill each other. It was very silly and very stupid, but it was a thing of pride. If you were challenged to a duel, you couldn't say no. You didn't want to let the family down, so you had to go and gamble your life away. You can do all things, but you don't need to prove yourself to the devil. That is a sign of low self-esteem. The Bible says that we should not tempt God. The devil told Adam and Eve that if they wanted to be like God and they wanted to be wise, they should eat the fruit. They should have said they were already like God and that they didn't need the fruit. The Holy Ghost gives us the ability and the grace to do the things we need to do.

UNDERSTANDING YOUR GIFTING: WITHIN GOD'S KINGDOM

Take time to understand how God has gifted you specifically for service. Are you a Pastor, a prophet, a teacher, an evangelist, or an apostle? The Spirit of God said to me that when the Spirit of God is moving in a place, each office responds to it differently. Understand how you are specifically gifted for service. When God is moving, a teacher will begin to understand different scriptures, and God will speak to them. One of my friends in a previous ministry would gather for specific tasks, and I would never like to be in his group. He would just talk and talk. The moment I realized he was an evangelist, I placed him in a different role.

KNOW YOUR PLACE

We can all learn anything, but the starting point is what we are naturally gifted in. We start from where we are, and then we can learn to covet other gifts and learn from other people. The moment you understand that God did not bring you to earth empty-handed, it boosts your confidence to know that your gift is needed. Each office comes with a group of gifts. Check out 1 Corinthians 12:7-11 and Romans 12. There are nine gifts that have been broken down into groups of three. In each office, there are some gifts that you will always find. For example, you can't say that you're in the prophetic office, and there is no word of knowledge or discernment at some level. It may be undeveloped, but it is there in some form.

You came with something to earth; you're not empty, and you're not useless. You are useful to the Body of Christ. So, don't compare yourself. If you do that, you'll never come out good. Either you will come out in pride, or you will come out with your esteem bruised. You'll never be the same. Please don't do it. Roman 12:3. The devil can give gifts too, but it's just like coffee, where it gives you something but takes something away in return. It's like going to borrow money from the mafia.

Only someone who loves themselves in the way God has ordained can truly love another person. Until you learn to love yourself, you cannot genuinely love someone else because you cannot give what you don't have. It might look like you're loving, but the truth is, it is selfish. Until you really love yourself, you can attempt to show love to people, but genuine love can only be given consistently when you love yourself. Sometimes people reject your love. But if you are confident in your love for yourself, you'll be able to manage those things properly.

God follows the same principle; He created the heavens and the earth. He made His home very beautiful. I've told people with terminal illnesses; that it's very difficult to get a glimpse and want to remain on earth. Don't feel guilty for resting. Don't feel guilty for pampering yourself every now and then. Don't feel guilty for turning off your phone and having me-time. It's something that needs to happen. If you take care of other people, there has to be a time when you pause to look after your own needs. You need to listen to your body but don't submit to your body. Know when you need to rest, when you need to be loved, and when you need to sleep. You need to have a gauge for those things because it's our duty to take care of this body. No one law of scripture should overshadow the other.

CARING FOR YOURSELF: YOUR BODY

Loving yourself is good, but knowing that your body should be cared for is still valid as well. There are many ways to take care of ourselves without violating scriptures, and loving yourself also includes taking care of the temple of the living God, which includes eating healthy. I once saw a video about completely cutting out sugar from your diet and all the benefits of that choice. While some things may be good for some people, you may have noticed that it's not the best for your own body, and that is part of taking care of and loving yourself.

At one point, the Lord told me to stop eating peanuts because they were bad for my eyes. Despite my love for them, I stopped eating them. Some people have no business eating cakes; loving and pampering yourself does not mean destroying your body. Organic food is more expensive than processed food for a reason, and, interestingly, the same people who say that organic food is expensive are the same people who buy $1000 phones.

CARING FOR YOURSELF: FRIENDSHIPS

It is not just food but also relationships, not only romantic but also friendships. You cannot be in toxic friendships where people constantly put you down and curse you. Loving yourself means cutting yourself off from toxic relationships, and you cannot let someone abuse you over the phone and stay on the line. Some people may say that it's rude, but the person abusing you is rude. These are ways that we can take care of ourselves.

Before we became friends, someone sent me nasty messages. I read the first line and saw where it was going, so I blocked the number and deleted the message. A few years later, she came to her senses and asked for forgiveness, and now we are friends and talk often. Pastors cannot hold grudges. Say out loud, "I love myself. I love others. But I love God more. Amen!" Anyone who makes you feel guilty for loving yourself is either ignorant or wicked, and to lead others, you need to love yourself. When I see a leader abusing people or leading people in a toxic way, I already know that this person does not love themselves. We have a responsibility to manage ourselves and to be able to lead at a higher level, you cannot be a sentimental person. You cannot be led by your feelings, as it will cause too many mistakes, push your friends away, and draw your enemies closer without you knowing it.

Look for Alignment

You may think some people are your best friends, but some might be close to you because of your money or connections. Some people judge their closeness to others based on the frequency of texts, calls, or invitations to events, but you want to ask yourself, "How has my life benefited from this friendship?" I gave someone an exercise to help them determine good friends, asking them which of their friends had ever asked about school and how it was going. After thinking for a moment, they realized that only a few had asked, and those were their true friends.

How many of your friends show interest in the things that really matter to you or at least get involved in them? Or is it all about partying? The COVID-19 pandemic has taught people, if they are paying attention, about the types of friends they have, and some people are beginning to realize that there is no basis for their friendship. It is sad that even in the Body of Christ, we have to be talking about clubs, but some people *still* club, and so we have to address it.

Pay Attention to When They Show Up

Some people only show up when something bad happens, as they need to sympathize, but when good things are happening, they're not there; they don't show up or celebrate with you, but they come to cry with you. If you are a sentimental person, you will think that the person is a good friend and is there for you. However, it has to be properly balanced, and when good things happen, they are nowhere to be found. You need to be able to sit down properly, rationally, and objectively think about these things. A sentimental person will hold onto that person because of how long they've known each other, and they don't stare the truth in the face, even though they know better.

This is one of the reasons some people say leadership is a lonely journey, but it doesn't have to be if we learn to assess friends objectively. It doesn't have to be lonely, but we must assess ourselves. When we decide in leadership, we need to know that we can't take everybody along. Some people will have to be left behind. All of that is part of loving yourself.

The moment I accepted the call to ministry, I knew my friends would have to reduce by at least 75%. It's a fact. The moment you start a business, or you are taking on an assignment in faith, or anything with sacrifice, you need to understand that those things have to change. Some people know that they have to shift from one group to another for the sake of their destiny, but they're too sentimental to do it. So, they are getting frustrated and angry, but they're still staying there. What am I saying? Take this step now. People will talk, but they won't talk for too long. People get distracted easily, and they will forget about you. Take this step for the sake of your destiny. When Jesus was going to step into ministry, he had to separate from His brothers.

Joseph

Another example is Joseph, who I love. He was sold into slavery and brought his brothers into Egypt, but if you read the story very closely, he wasn't associated with them in Egypt. He wasn't going to hang out with Judah and Simeon and say, "What's up?" No, things had already changed. They would have begun to try and rule Egypt through him because they were his big brothers. That is why, when their father died, they feared that Joseph would treat them partially. But he met with them in Goshen and said they shouldn't be afraid. And then he went back to the palace. He ruled for eighty years scandal-free, starting at 30 and dying at 110 years old. If you are going to lead at a higher level, you cannot lead sentimentally.

Moses

Moses' ministry would have been destroyed because of Aaron, his brother. Not being sentimental means that you see the truth in front of you. I am not saying that you should go and cut people off and move to an island. Absolutely not; I am simply saying that you can choose which friendships deepen and which friendships to give yourself space from. The moment your value is being trampled upon, that is some form of abuse. It may not be that the person is doing it intentionally, but it's still being done. You are no longer needed but still forcing yourself to be there. We need to know when we have overstayed our welcome in a relationship or friendship.

LOVING OTHERS

1 John 4:7, *"Beloved, let us love one another, for love is of God; and everyone who loves is born of God and knows God."*

Why is it hard for Christians of the opposite sex to say that they love each other without a sexual connotation? It is emotional immaturity. That's why we often say "I love you" to each other at CCCG. People's mindsets have been corrupted. When you were much younger and told your parents that you loved them, did you have sex in mind? Definitely not, but as you went through life, you were exposed to different things, and suddenly, everything became deranged. So we are going back to that place of purity of relationships. That's what the Bible says we should do.

I'll take a moment to say that liking someone is different from loving them. What the world is teaching is about liking people. However, what the Bible teaches is about loving people. Liking someone means that you're admiring something in someone so that emotional response is born out of admiration for something.

The Bible says that there is a higher level called love where you can do things that show you like them even though you don't admire anything in them because it is a decision. 'Likeness' is born out of affection and feelings, while love is born of a decision. I can give you money because I like you and do the things I like, but I can still give you money because God told me to give you money, or you're in need even though you're doing things I don't like. That's the difference.

DISARMING HATRED THROUGH LOVE

Some people only show affection towards black people like them or towards people from their narrow-minded tribe or from their country. They act in a derogatory way to everybody else, but the moment they see someone from their country, even if that person is a murderer, they get excited. I just think to myself, what kind of human being is this? That's not the way it is supposed to be.

Do you know something interesting? Christians do this a lot. You may be friends with someone, talking to them about a lot of things, but the moment you realize that the person is gay, you change your countenance. You were friends, and everything was good, but then all of a sudden, once you've got this new information, they just look very dirty to you, and you're irritated by them. So my first question is, where was your discernment in the beginning?

This is why it's difficult for many homosexuals to come to Christ. I see the hatred that Christians show them. And God forbid if I were even in that state, how would I come to a Christ like that? You say God is love, yet you behave differently. If the same people realize someone is an adulterer, they still remain friends with that person. But because someone else is in a same-sex relationship, they would consider them to be bad people. Am I condoning this? Absolutely not. Just like I don't condone lying, pornography, fornication, adultery, or any of those sins. They're all in the same category, but some of us have fallen into the trap of elevating homosexuality above every other sin, but we still expect them to run to Christ.

That's why Jesus came to the earth and used love to disarm many people. The Samaritan woman being one of them. She came to fetch water at the time of day because she couldn't come in the morning and the evening because the other women would be there at that time, and she had slept with most of their husbands. But Jesus associated with her, and she was shocked because she was a Samaritan and He was a Jew. Historically, Jews and Samaritans don't mix, but love disarmed her. How far should we go in showing love to them without crossing the line to accept what they're doing? We love people, but we hate their sins. Even I, as a Pastor, and the people in this wonderful, would find it very difficult to treat people according to their mistakes.

Do you know what got Ananias and Sapphira killed? Lying. Do you know how many people have lied to me before? In their head, they had justifications. And even when I confronted them, they still lied. We hate sin, but we love people. It is very difficult to separate the two sometimes, but the more we do it, the better we will get at separating those things. I know a homosexual who attended Cornerstone; he left the province but occasionally connects with us. I speak with and counsel him, but I don't talk about homosexuality.

The strange thing is that, because of the abuse that the community has experienced from Christians, a lot of what drives them is hate - the hate they've received. Of course, their actions are bad, but that's not our focus. Whenever they come close to a Pastor, they first want to put out there quickly that they're gay. They want to tell you immediately so you can just hate them like everyone else.

A guy reached out to me; he heard the sermon I preached titled, "I Am Different." He is a transgender - born a woman, converted, and became a man. He is of African origin. He had been ostracized by his family, and he heard the message. In the message, I referenced Adam and Eve. Here, I explained that the original Adam had both male and female inside him, but the female aspect was taken out to create a separate entity. God performed surgery on the first man.

I was saying that sometimes people can come to the earth as both male and female and sometimes surgery is needed to remove Eve from that combined entity. He said that when he heard that, he felt loved again. We met and spoke about those things. It's very sad that when people like that come, our first reaction is to change them from being gay to being straight as if that's the only thing people need. So sometimes, I don't even touch on that for years, except God leads me to. Similarly, I would do the same for someone who is straight but addicted to pornography; I will still minister to them.

We are called to love. I can't fathom a regular business stating that they can't render service to someone because they're homosexual. However, I wouldn't marry them because I would be joining them as one, and the Bible does not condone that. So based on scripture, I cannot do that. In the same way, many have also experienced hatred in the form of racism.

Does a white person have to love a black person? No, they don't. Don't be under any illusion. But there's a way that some of them are treated that makes you know that their activism is pure hatred. That's how I see many Christians treat people, especially same-sex people. I won't march with them because I don't believe in what they are doing, but the love I have for them oozes to them, and they are drawn to me because they know I don't judge them. If we do talk about that, it's because they want to talk about it, and I tell them what the Bible says. I love them too much to keep this away from them.

Many people think that the only reason why people are gay is that they are just playing around, but people don't understand that it cuts across different layers. There are some physiological reasons why those things come to life. If you have heard of crack babies, those are babies who have an addiction to crack or cocaine because, in the womb, it flowed into the baby from the mother who was using drugs. A pregnant woman can take certain medications, and the doctors might tell her to stop taking those medications if she becomes pregnant. In those cases, continuing the medication could alter the baby's physiological makeup if not stopped. When you see a grown person tell you they really feel in a particular way, don't discard it and say they are just a sinner. That is insensitive and wicked. For some people, it was a spiritual attack or a physiological alteration that happened before birth.

I will tell you a story. When I moved to Toronto from Europe, I was living with another member of the church that I attended in Nigeria. I was there for about three months, but there was a day that suddenly, I looked at a man and began to be attracted to him. I thought, "What nonsense is this?" The thoughts would just come. I kept rebuking and rebuking them. The thoughts would go away, but then randomly, after a few days, those same thoughts crossed my mind again. I wondered where these nonsense thoughts came from and shut them down.

One day I was having a casual conversation with my uncle, and he briefly said that the previous owners of the house I was staying in were a gay couple. That's when I understood that the couple most likely had a spiritual component controlling their same-sex lifestyle. I was not a Pastor then, but I was still walking with God and knew enough to rebuke the thoughts and stand my ground. But imagine a little child, a young boy, or a young girl. Imagine that spirit coming to attack a young person, not just in age but also in the spirit. They would just have those ideas about the lifestyle, and they would begin to explore with friends. Once they find themselves exploring, they suddenly realize that they are gay. It could be physiological because of medications; it could be spiritual, and it can also be emotional.

We as a Movement (church) need to understand these things about same-sex relationships so that if we are dealing with someone who became homosexual, we'll be properly equipped to lead or counsel. Somebody else in the church was married and started experiencing feelings for the same sex. Although the person had been shutting it down, they now needed assistance. I didn't judge the person; we are working together to deal with this and asked God to give that person grace to be able to handle and stand their ground. This is an individual with kids, but those feelings were present.

Instead of hatred, compassion must go ahead of us. There's zero judgment if I'm dealing with someone who got into same-sex relationships because of physiological imbalances. If they want to see a change, I will work with them. God heals the sick. He can also heal them, and they may wake up and realize that they no longer have an attraction to the same sex. We are called to love people. We don't have to accept what they're doing, but we are called to love them.

DEMONSTRATING LOVE FOR OTHERS

Accept Them

How do we demonstrate love for other people? We accept them. Our first thing when we meet with people is not how we can change the person. That's what colonialism tried to do, and that was bad. The focus was on how I could change this person.

Some of us come from those types of cultures, and we are not happy about it, but now that we have power, we want to colonize other people. Even in some of our friendships, we're trying to change people, and that is our agenda, so we're colonial masters without knowing it. It's different when somebody says that they need help, and you're working together. You take it upon yourself because you think the person is bad; that is not healthy. Accept people for who they are. In my mind, if they never change, I would still be okay with that. We just may not be best friends. If you are okay with yourself, then I'm comfortable with that.

Some people are loud, some people are quiet. When the messages are going on in CCCG, it's typically quiet. However, when some new members who were more expressive began to come, they would speak up during services. For example, they would say things like, "Preach on Pastor!" etc. Some other people were irritated by this, but I shut down their comments because everyone is welcome at CCCG. At the end of the day, God made all of us, and we are all different.

Love is a decision, and loving people is the quickest way to mature. I have understood that not everybody will be like me. I understand that I am not a perfect picture of how a perfect human being should act. I understand that I have my strengths and areas I'm still growing. When I look at people, I don't just see their weaknesses. I look for their strengths. It helps me balance the obnoxiousness and bad habits I see and all those other things.

Recognize People's Needs

This is particularly important for leaders. As a Pastor, there are some people who don't need me calling them every day. In fact, they would see it as a bother. On the other hand, some people want or need daily communication. Therefore, we lead people by recognizing their individual needs. My leadership style is to tell people what I want them to do and the vision, and then I leave them alone. I believe that if they need help, they will come back to me. If they don't come back to me, I expect everything to be perfect by the deadline. However, some people might feel that I hate or have abandoned them if I lead them that way. Some people prefer to give daily updates just to get feedback.

As leaders, we must recognize and work with people's needs. I can't force my leadership style on everybody; that is unfair. Keep in mind that people's needs can change. For example, someone who has just come out of a traumatic experience or relationship may not want to be touched or have people come close to them. Instead, they might want to be spoken to from afar. We need to respect that because certain things could remind them of where they just came from. Some of these people might be in groups we lead in church or the secular world.

I was privileged to lead the delegation for the shelters for survivors of domestic abuse. Men are typically not allowed there, but God mercifully allowed me to minister to those women. There was a reason why men weren't allowed there because it reminded them of the trauma they went through. So when dealing with them, I give them a healthy space. Sometimes you talk to people, and they come very close to you while speaking. You don't deal with people who have suffered abuse in that way, except those who have already gotten over it. So, I give them enough space. If they want to come closer because they're more comfortable, then I respond in that way. We need to be self-aware as leaders. Who am I dealing with? What exactly do they need? If you give someone more than what they need, it can become abusive.

The Bible says that if you wake up early in the morning blessing your neighbour, it can be taken as a curse. If you wake up very early and begin to shout, "God bless my neighbour! May you prosper in Jesus' name!" it would be considered a curse, so you keep it to yourself unless they invite you for a prayer meeting. Recognize people's spiritual needs, emotional needs, personal needs, and physical needs.

HOW TO LOVE PEOPLE BETTER

Ask People About Their Needs

One of the best ways of doing that is by asking them how you can help them. Sometimes people just want to give me an update, but they are not asking for help. Simple questions can prevent so many hurts. Offering something that ends up being rejected will now hurt you as a leader, and the next thing you know, the devil will tell you that you're not being accepted and nobody loves you. So, ask them how you can help them and what kind of assistance they need. One of the members of our church lost their dad. We visited and asked him how we could assist him. He let us know what was needed, and we accommodated. The point is one of the ways to love people is by asking them what they need, and you will see if you can meet their needs, or not.

Pray for Them

Another way to love people is by praying for them. I remember on December 31st, 2018, I was lying down on the couch, meditating and preparing for our Crossover Service, when the Lord said to me that the more you pray for someone, the more you bond with them. I found that very interesting because I had never known that before. Some people don't know why they love their Pastor so much, but it's because of the prayers. One day, when I was in another ministry, I had a dream and saw my Pastor kneeling down by my side, praying for me. Of course, he wouldn't come and tell me that he was praying for me, but the bond was there.

So, we should pray for people without telling them that we are praying for them. God knows what we're doing in secret. Parents should pray for their kids. I remember many times in the middle of the night, I would feel my dad's hand on my head while sleeping. He did that many times while we were growing up. There are many reasons why, even though we did many bad things, we didn't go crazy. A lot of it was because of love and respect. Sometimes, when I wanted to go crazy, I would think twice because of love. Look at your prayer lists and ask yourself if the prayers are just for yourself, your family, and your kids. Add other people to the prayer list. Pray for your Pastors, church, city, and others, not just your family members.

In 2021, we had the first meeting of the School of Prophets for those in the prophetic office, and I was explaining to them among other things that the primary job of a prophet is intercession. When you perceive, see, or hear something, the main reason is so that you can pray, not just feel things. When you connect with or greet someone, and you sense heaviness, pray for that person. Strengthen people, make way for them, pray in the spirit, and the burden that you feel will lift. You will hear the testimony later. The moment you embody these three different forms of love for God, self, and others, suddenly, leadership becomes a joyful experience and not a painful experience or chore.

LEADING WITH LOVE: WHEN PEOPLE HURT YOU

Do people hurt me as a leader? Yes, you bet, beyond what people can imagine. When it comes, it comes very strongly, but will we stop loving? No, never. Some people have come before and said that God sent them to CCCG. We corrected them once, and they didn't pick up our calls again. They said that God was leading them somewhere else. Some people borrowed money from us, promised to pay us back, then left the church and started to speak evil about us, but they didn't talk about the fact that they borrowed money from us and didn't repay. We knew, but we just kept it quiet.

If you think that you are going to lead and everybody will love you because you love them, that is an illusion. You would be in dreamland. That is normal, and it happened to Jesus. That shouldn't make you stop loving people. It's normal, so why would you want to stop loving people? The more you love even when you're being hurt, the more the anointing on your life grows.

Ask Moses. It grows and grows. Moses' brother and sister spoke against him, and God wanted to punish them, but Moses was still begging on their behalf. Why was he doing that? Because he was a wise man. David said something in the book of Psalms. He said that when

God is punishing your enemies, don't rejoice because He could see you rejoicing over your enemies and may stop punishing them.

Seek Emotional Support

We are leaders, and we will keep leading and loving. If you know you've been hurt before, you may need to take some time to get counselling. Sometimes you may need to speak to someone to help you deal with the wounds of leadership. Sometimes it is necessary.

I remember meeting with the former president of Vanguard College, and we were talking when he asked me a question. He asked, "How much do you love your congregation?" I asked him to elaborate, and he said, "On a scale from one to ten." I said, "100%." He asked me how it was possible and whether they had hurt me. He mentors many Pastors and is used to all the stories of the hurts and disappointment. I said to him, "You know, Sir, maybe I'm naive. But I'm not in ministry for people. I am an administrator for God, and I'm serving the people on behalf of God." He looked at me as if I had no idea, and the conversation shifted at that point.

I know what God does in every service, and if my expectation is that people would appreciate me and do special things for me, then I would be disappointed. However, that's not my expectation. My expectation is, 'God, did I do what you wanted me to do?' If He says yes, then I'm good. Whether people say that I had a great message or did not have a great message, it genuinely means nothing to me. When I kneel down at my seat after each message, I pray in the Spirit, and I get that assurance in my spirit that I am doing well. I stand up like a boss because I have been validated by my boss, and that is all that matters.

MEASURING YOUR GROWTH IN LOVE

You can measure your love by how easily you get irritated by people, yourself, and the speed at which God moves. The irritation is a proper measurement of your growth in love in all those areas. When I started out in ministry, I would look at people and get frustrated at their behaviour. But as I grew in love, I realized that though that person hasn't changed, I still love them. In the same way, you know physically that there's a problem like headaches, joint pains, or fever, and understanding that something is going on with your health is the same way you would monitor the irritation to measure your growth in love.

10

Emotional Intelligence

When you think of a perfect leader, what traits come to mind? Leaders have patience, they are calm under pressure, they are honest, and they have clear and good communication. Leaders are people of integrity, they are adaptable, and they are problem solvers. They don't have to be the ones solving the problems themselves, but they can coordinate solving the problems. They show impartiality and don't have favourites. They are empathetic, service-oriented, decisive, and good listeners and have a vision. Not only do they have a vision, but they also have the ability to follow through on a vision. They're humble, reliable, even-tempered, generous, discerning, disciplined, and continually strive for excellence.

Who is a leader? You might picture someone who never lets their temper get out of control no matter what problems they're facing or someone who has complete trust in the people working with them and delegates tasks. They're disciplined, confident, and listen to others. They are easy to talk to and make careful, educated decisions. All these things can be encapsulated in emotional intelligence.

Emotional intelligence is the ability to understand and manage your own emotions and those of the people around you. That seems like a very simple definition, but when we understand that many things are controlled by emotional responses, the definition begins to make more sense. When people slip up or mess up, many times, it is because they are good people, but something was not managed the way it was supposed to have been managed.

Every one of us is here on this earth, and as long as we are here, we are interacting based on the flesh, which is our body, our minds, and our emotions. Many times, the way people know that they are getting to you is based on your emotional response. People with a high degree of emotional intelligence know what their feelings are at every point in time. Some people would tell you to just forget about your feelings. What the well-meaning people are trying to say is not to let your feelings control you.

We must be aware of our feelings. So, emotionally intelligent people know their feelings, what those feelings mean, and how they can affect others. They know what they are feeling and what the feelings mean. They know where those feelings came from, and they know how those emotions can affect other people. Some people were brought up by people who have a high degree of emotional intelligence. These parents raised their kids to express their feelings instead of throwing temper tantrums.

For leaders, having high emotional intelligence is essential for success. Nobody wants to be led by someone who cannot control themselves or whose behaviour they can't predict. The followers don't know what they are going to be met with each day. So people can enjoy being around those types of leaders until they find a place that is safe for them to be.

If you have not read the book, "Emotional Intelligence 2.0" by Travis Bradberry and Jean Greaves, I would recommend you read it. It would help those who have a solid background in the faith. They drew inspiration from scriptures. For those who study psychology, you would know that psychology actually originated from the church. They just removed Christ from it, and certain types of people came into the picture to add interesting theories, and you know how the story goes. There are five key aspects of emotional intelligence:

1. **Self-Awareness**
2. **Self-Regulation**
3. **Motivation**
4. **Empathy**
5. **Social Skills**

The more we manage ourselves in these areas, our emotional intelligence will increase. We cannot get rid of our emotional responses as long as we are on this earth, and God's design is not for us to function without them, as that would lead to a dry and boring life.

SELF - AWARENESS

If you are self-aware, you will always know how you feel and understand how your emotions and actions affect the people around you. Being self-aware means having a clear picture of our strengths and weaknesses. I see self-awareness as loving yourself so you know yourself. Jesus demonstrated self-awareness as our ultimate Master and Leader. (Matthew 26:38) People who are not emotionally intelligent will deny how they feel, pretending that everything is fine, which can make them untrustworthy. If people cannot see your emotions, they cannot trust you. The Bible tells us that Jesus was in tune with the way He felt. (John 11:33-35)

Some people fear demonstrating excitement because they think people will look down on them. Others only show anger because it keeps people away and makes them feel respected. Moses did the same thing in Numbers 11:1-12. On the one hand, having a leader who thinks everything you do wrong is okay is not great. On the other hand, a leader should not always condemn people and nail them to the cross for doing wrong. Instead, a leader should tell them that they are not pleased with what they did. We have to start with identification. If we feel angry, we must acknowledge it.

My book, "A Disciplined Life", has a chapter on disciplined emotions. If God gave us emotions, they're not bad. For example, the Bible says it's okay to be angry but not to sin in the process. Is that not clear enough? In many cases, people are condemned for being angry and raised with that kind of condemnation and judgment. No wonder they bottle it up, and then suddenly, there are outbursts of explosions. If people are raised to understand that it's okay to be angry because it's an emotional response and are taught how to manage their anger, there won't be a need for outbursts of anger. Anger is like boiling water in a pot. When it reaches boiling point, it begins to push the lid. You can push the lid away depending on your boiling point. But if there are holes in the lid designed to help the steam escape, then you won't need to push the lid away. Being angry, happy, frustrated, excited, or sorrowful is okay. The Bible says to rejoice with those who are rejoicing and mourn with those who are mourning.

IMPROVING SELF-AWARENESS

Journalling

By writing out what happened during the day and how you felt about those events, you can discipline yourself to identify your emotions. There's an interesting phenomenon. Why do many people feel happy or relieved when they see a psychologist? It's because the psychologist helps them identify their emotions when certain circumstances happen and explore them. People leave feeling at peace and relieved.

Can you imagine someone who has been living on earth for five years and has never gone to the washroom? That's how many people are emotionally. They have all of this emotional waste they have been carrying around, making them like a truck whose brakes have failed. It's better to avoid them unless you have the anointing to stop them. Otherwise, they're looking for the slightest opportunity and who to unload on because it's not a regular thing.

Everyone has different bowel movements. If we use the physical to understand the emotional, we can see that some people use the bathroom twice a day, some once a day, and some maybe once or twice a week. Whenever I see a problem that persists even after prayer and fasting, I ask God quite a number of questions. Most likely, there are principles that are being broken. This is part of what led us to the decision to add emotional intelligence to this course. You can see some good people consistently making bad mistakes and start to wonder what's wrong with that person. An average person might look at them and think that it is demonic activity. But in many cases, it's at the emotional management level. Of course, if the person gives the enemy an entry point, like offence, the enemy can come in and become demonic.

For many people, anger begins as just an emotional thing. For example, let's say that you asked for water, and you asked for cold water. Let's say that someone didn't hear the instruction of cold and just came with warm water. You are thirsty because it's hot outside, and you know you emphasized that you wanted cold water, but you got warm water. You need to be self-aware enough to know that there was a disappointment because you clearly expressed that it needed to be cold. Being self-aware is acknowledging that something changed on the inside of you. You were cool, and everything was good, but suddenly you just have an attitude. Being able to identify the point where an attitude or change in emotions started is defined by self-awareness. Keeping journals will help us pay attention to these things and help us track them until it becomes a lifestyle.

When we started to get used to the discipline of devotions, some of us had it on our calendars and reminders. Some have reached the point where they don't need external reminders. When they wake up daily, they know they have to spend time with God.

Slowing Down

The second way we can improve our self-awareness is by slowing down. The pace at which many people are going makes them miss out on so many things. When you experience anger and realize that something is off, take a deep breath and figure out what you're feeling. When I talk to some people, for example, and they're describing their feelings as 'weird' or 'off,' I ask them what weird means. Weird is not an emotion.

Do you feel uncomfortable, threatened, uncomfortable, ashamed, or humiliated? What exactly are you feeling? The devil thrives in ignorance, so the more ignorant a person is, the more the likelihood of them remaining bound. When we talked about the twelve demonic governments, we talked about how to deal with spirits; we need to identify them. Jesus did this all the time - "You deaf-and-dumb spirit." Slow down and evaluate why you're feeling that emotion. You need to be humble enough to acknowledge that you may have been rude when reacting to people.

Proud people will just say that someone else gave them an attitude, and they would miss an opportunity to learn. Remember, no matter the situation, you can always choose how to react to it, but first, you must learn how to identify your feelings. You were fine until a text message came in from a particular person. Suddenly, you started feeling uncomfortable or out of breath and angry. Why? First of all, identify what actually happened, and then dig deep and determine why that happened.

The next question from myself and the Holy Ghost is, "Why?" Exuberance can make a person respond in a particular way. How do you moderate your peace? Perhaps we should be saying that when you notice something has shifted, discipline yourself to pause at that time and identify it. If we don't deal with it immediately as a negative interaction, it will spread to others, and your reputation will also suffer.

Let's say you're driving to church, and you're happy and singing, but then someone cuts you off. Next, you begin to vent about how Edmonton has bad drivers. You didn't identify that something had changed and stopped singing. When you arrived at church, the ushers smiled at you and said hello, but you ignored them and walked straight in.

So now, the interactions have been messed up, and you're not giving people the opportunity to help you or get to know who you truly are.

What we're talking about does not just happen overnight. It's like what working out does to the body. You can't master it by going to the gym once for nine hours. It is more challenging to manage emotions than to manage the body. So in the order of challenge, the body is the easiest, then you move to the emotions, then the mind, and the will. Then you move to the spiritual aspect, which will take a lifetime and beyond to master.

SELF - REGULATION

Self-regulation is about staying in control. It's about knowing that it is cold outside, knowing where the thermostat is, knowing the temperature you want to be at, and adjusting the temperature accordingly. We can go deeper into that analogy by saying that you can set it based on different times. In the morning, a different kind of temperature is required than in the afternoons, and the night is different. For example, there are some cold phone calls you will not receive at certain times based on what you know about your regulation. This covers a leader's flexibility and commitment to personal accountability.

Anybody can get angry because someone was rude to them. Any Tom, Dick, and Harry can do that; even a child can do that. Paul said that when he was a child, he behaved like a child. If you're nice to a child, the child is nice to you, but if you're rude to a child, the child can also be rude to you. They don't really have the ability to self-regulate. If they want to pee, they pee where they are. That is the same thing on the emotional level with quite a few people. The way they feel is just the way they give it. In many cases, it's because they don't know what they're feeling in the first place, and the only way they get feedback is after they have responded and people give them feedback. It is almost like asking someone else to be your mirror. So if you dress up, the best way to know you look good is by having someone else tell you that you look good instead of having your own mirror where you can check for yourself and adjust properly before you step out. This is where the bulk of the work is in self-regulation.

IMPROVING SELF-REGULATION

Know Your Value

Your values must be driven by principles. For example, as a child of God, I am an ambassador of Christ every time I go out, and there is a particular way I am expected to behave. This applies not only to being a child of God but also to being a Pastor. While others may get angry, throw a fit, and destroy things, it's different for a Pastor. People can curse at the workplace, but the moment *you* curse, they say, "Oh well! And you call yourself a Christian?" It's not fair, but that's the way it is. Knowing your values and the lines you will not cross is essential.

Do you have an idea of where you will never compromise? You can do anything you want, but you have to know the line you will never cross because of your principles. You don't need anyone's permission to follow your principles. Do you know what values are most important to you? Spend time examining your code of ethics. What would you never do? Someone can be rude to you and make you angry, but you won't yell because those are your principles. It has nothing to do with what people will think of you; it's your principles. In line with scripture, there are ways we can respond to things that even God will approve of. If you know what's most important to you, you probably won't have to think twice when you face a moral or ethical decision. It starts with knowing your values.

Hold Yourself Accountable

If you always blame others when you're angry, you're not holding yourself accountable. "Why did you pee on the bed?" "Because you gave me water to drink last night." It makes no sense. If you tend to blame others when something goes wrong, stop it now. That's not becoming of a leader. Make a commitment to admit your mistakes and face the consequences. Whether someone was screaming or not, it doesn't matter; hold yourself to higher standards than other people. "I am responsible for my own response." That's the principle of being proactive, as opposed to being reactive.

Make a commitment to admit your mistakes and face the consequences, whatever they are. One of the ways you can quickly spot a leader in a group of people who have done something wrong is by identifying their responses when they are being corrected. "It wasn't me; it wasn't me!" That's one response. Or "It wasn't my fault; this person made me do it." These are both responses we should never emulate. "I was there, and I take responsibility for being there, and I am sorry." That's a leader; we hold ourselves accountable. Yes. That person's actions might have contributed, but you still hold yourself to the standard.

Let's say two kids are fighting, and you go to one of them and ask, "What happened? Why are you beating them up?" "Because he slapped me." That's the wrong answer. You're beating him up because you want to beat him up! The slap just motivated you. Because you could have been slapped and said that you would turn the other cheek. The child could have also turned around and gone in different directions! Reframe these things.

Jesus and His disciples were going to Jerusalem. They decided to pass through a particular city, but they didn't accept Him in this city, and the disciples became angry. Jesus said it was fine and wanted to go. The disciples wanted to call down fire from heaven. Why did they want to call down fire from heaven? They were vengeful. What really got to them? It was the feeling of rejection. They were having self-confidence and pride issues. It's different sides of the same coin. Anyone who lacks self-confidence is most likely walking in pride. To them, they have so much power that they could never be rejected again, but they were rejected and decided that these people must pay for it. That was their line of thinking.

I am emphasizing the point of taking full responsibility for all of your actions. A person can beat or slap you, but it doesn't necessarily mean you have to respond that way. We have the right to decide how we respond. We need to get to a point where we are fully in charge of what we do and what we don't do without deferring responsibility to anyone else. It's a lot to ask, which is why we are leaders. The leaders who will excel do not behave like everybody else. Down the line, the person will look back and realize that the person is a woman or man of God. We should not be holding grudges. I am responsible for how I respond to people.

In the book, "The Blessings of Being Under Spiritual Authority", I said that you should read the whole book before applying what you've learned. This is one of the reasons why. If you just heard 'turn the other cheek' you would become a doormat, which is not what God ordained. The same Jesus who overturned the tables is the same one who said to turn the other cheek. Jesus is both the 'Lion and the Lamb.'

Practice Being Calm

The next time you're in a challenging situation, be very aware of how you're acting. The Lord said to me a few years ago that if I lived my life as if I was in a reality TV show, knowing that He watches me everywhere I go, it would help me live a holy life. Imagine banks where there are cameras everywhere, and the teller steals money. It's just very silly. A few minutes afterward, someone would tap them and ask if they could see that someone was watching them.

Some people relieve their stress by shouting at people when they're frustrated. They take it out on others. You can practice breathing and count from 1 to 100 or whatever works for you. You just need to give yourself enough time to calm down, and that is usually the issue. The moment something bad happens, take a moment to calm down before responding.

There is a book about Abraham Lincoln I once read. Whenever he was angry, he would write damning letters to people, but his wife would take and destroy them. There was a time when he actually thought he had posted a letter to a general who messed up. The wife ended up writing a different letter, and he was shocked at how the general had responded because he didn't know she had written him something. You can write all the angry things you want to say to someone and just tear it up. Whatever works for you. Like using the washroom, you feel lighter when you pour feelings of anger. But if you do it inappropriately, the heaviness will multiply, especially for someone with principles.

I often bring myself back to earth and remind myself that what I am focused on will not take me to heaven. Comparing it to heaven makes what seemed like a huge thing suddenly become irrelevant, just a little thing. Though I have had many opportunities to be angry at many people, there are things we can practice that make it easier for us to lead and for others to follow us because they feel safe around us. The next point is to vent and receive counsel.

One of the best ways to vent is to vent to God, but some people do not do it well. Let's continue with the bathroom analogy. You're pressed, you go to the washroom, sitting on the toilet bowl for 30 minutes, nothing comes out, and then you get up and go on with your day. Did you actually have a release? Venting to God is one of the most effective ways to vent, and David did a lot of it. If you read Psalms 69, you will see the way he was venting to God. Without understanding, the devil can easily convince you that you are being disrespectful to God. David was a man who God said was after His own heart. If you do not feel like David, you do not need to talk like him. Psalms 69:1-6 is an example of venting, and David went on and on to God. By Verse 12, David noticed the citizens gossiping but did not keep it to himself. He went to God with all the burdens and left them in His presence, pouring them out to God. Moses did the same thing. Some people might need it more frequently than others, like a bowel movement. We are all built differently, and some people may not have the need to vent for one or two years. You know yourself, so do not feel guilty and compare yourself. If your bowels are full, go and release it. That way, when stepping out to lead people, you are leading from a place of love and overflow.

Venting vs Complaining

What is the difference between venting and complaining? Excellent question; I am glad you asked! If you read Psalms 69, you can see the difference there. Venting is talking and allowing God's wisdom to influence your decisions and conclusions. The person complaining is not listening to someone else's advice or wise counsel. They just want to talk and go back to what they believe. That is complaining. Your receptiveness to God's counsel is what will determine if you are venting or complaining. If you are venting, you will leave the presence of God refreshed, but if you are complaining, you will go back the same way you came. Let's look at some examples.

Numbers 11

They were complaining because they had no food. They needed food, and they needed water. What is venting? "Lord, you brought us out, and we were just eating manna, and there's nothing else to eat, but we know that you're the provider, and we know that you can make everything available for us." What is complaining? Crying is a sign of hopelessness. Moses also complained in that same chapter." He asked, "Why have you given me all these people? And you didn't send any help? Can you claim you love me?" God did not kill Moses.

Why? Because Moses was not complaining, he was venting. Someone complaining will not accept a solution. They don't want to; they just want to talk.

David & Samuel

Let's look at David and Samuel in 1 Samuel 19:18-20. It's not only God we can vent to. When we are upset with God, we are actually upset with our perception of God. In theory, David ran away from Saul. Why are we using this as an example? Saul represented God to the Israelis as a king, but Samuel also represented God to the Israelis as a prophet. This question covers both God and spiritual authority. When it comes to venting, we should only vent to someone who is part of the problem or part of the solution. Otherwise, it becomes glorified venting, which is gossip and maligns the person's character.

What are we trying to say? Some people may have an issue with an individual in the church and vent to a friend or a family member about that situation. The problem is that when the issue is resolved, they won't go back and tell the same person that the issue has been resolved and that an individual is actually a good person. They have now planted a seed in the family member or friend's mind. We don't do that; this is part of self-regulation. You might be frustrated with someone, but everything you say must be limited to those who are part of the solution.

Ministry

Let's give more practical examples. Someone is serving in the Music ministry, another is serving in the Audio-Visual ministry, and someone is in the Continuous Improvement ministry. But say there is miscommunication or a challenge. There is no need for the leader of the Music ministry to tell a member of the Music ministry what a member of the Continuous Improvement ministry is doing. Even though the member may give good advice because they're a child of God, the principle has been broken because the member of the Music ministry has nothing to do with it. You can go and speak with the leader of the Continuous Improvement ministry or the person the member reports to.

If someone has kidney failure, they may not be able to hold their own pee. In the same way, someone who has been traumatized emotionally can have difficulty regulating themselves when they go through these types of situations. When something happens, they may misunderstand and read meaning into it. They may have an elaborate conspiracy theory that seems right to them but may not be 100% true. So they need to hold it in.

There are times when I have gone to my spiritual father to talk about certain challenges that I've experienced with some people in ministry. I could tell him because he was part of the solution, a person I could draw from, someone I report to and whose authority I'm under. I told him what I had gone through, asked him if he'd gone through that before, and asked for his advice. He gave me counsel and told me what he believed I should do. I did it, and everything worked well. I don't need to tell another leader in another ministry about my problem because they have nothing to do with it. So if they ask me how things are, I just say things are excellent, things are good. If someone asks you how you are and you say you need to pee, that's the way a child would respond. That is self-regulation. The sky is not falling.

Relationships

How would you apply these things with your spouse or significant other? Certain principles govern the way things work, and there are certain scenarios where it is appropriate to involve a spouse. The Bible says that two shall become one, but if you work for the CIA, you can't necessarily use this as an excuse to divulge confidential information, especially if that information may harm your spouse or their spouse.

It becomes tricky because, in many circumstances, even a spouse has nothing to do with the solution. An exception may be if the person is in immediate danger. I see this from the perspective of protecting the other person. In many cases, negative things are involved, and you may be transmitting offence or negative things to the spouse that they don't need to be involved in. The assumption is that we are dealing with mature people.

Let's say someone called me a fool. I don't need to tell my wife because now I am introducing her to the possibility of walking in offense. After I've dealt with the person, will I go back and say that I hope my wife has dealt with the offense? You are just spreading those things around. This is a part of self-regulation. I can deal with that on my own. If she is part of the problem or part of the solution, I will bring her into the situation. I can see one or two scenarios where the spouse could be brought on board if they're mature enough. The assumption is that the man and the woman are mature enough. The same thing happens with siblings as well. They fight with one person, and now the whole gang comes to fight you.

Everything will be fine if you do things through the proper channels. For example, if someone is coming to you and complaining about someone else, you have to assess why you are being brought into the situation. If you realize that it doesn't have anything to do with you, redirect them to the people with a direct hand in solving the problem.

In my case, even as the lead Pastor, if someone who serves in a particular ministry in the church comes directly to me, I will ask that person if they have gone to their ministry leader first and if that leader is aware. If the leader is not aware, I redirect them to talk to the leader first. If it's a situation that has to do with the ministry leader, like harassment, for example, they cannot report to the ministry leader in that case; they would come to me, and then we would take appropriate steps to resolve it. So we have touched on self-awareness and self-regulation. The emphasis is on the self. So, as a leader, it is my job to regulate myself. It is my call to calm myself down.

MOTIVATION

As a matter of principle, every group must be led by somebody. One person must own it. It is that person who owns the responsibility and needs to be aware of the challenge, and it becomes the responsibility of that individual to look for the solution.

One of the ways that people we lead can get frustrated is when the leader is not motivated, always dropping the ball, making consistent mistakes, and being passive in leadership. Being in a position but not making any change. If we keep doing the same things repeatedly, no matter who we are, we become a bit disillusioned, asking ourselves why we're doing what we're doing. You will have seasons where you question your relationship with God. To avoid looking back, you will have to refresh yourself on why you are doing what you're doing. This is what happened to Elijah when he said, "It is enough! Now Lord, take my life, for I am no better than my fathers!" God gave him a fresh assignment to anoint Hazel, Jehu, and Elisha.

Self-motivated leaders consistently work toward their goals. One of the evilest things that I've seen is to be led by a leader who is not motivated, does not want to do anything, and will not allow you to do anything. John Maxwell said that you could only go as far as the leader who is leading you. Everything rises and falls on leadership.

IMPROVING YOUR MOTIVATION

Examine why you're doing what you're doing. It can be a secular or ministry job; re-evaluate it and re-examine it regularly. In my case, most of the time when I have retreats, I re-evaluate these things. Why did God establish Cornerstone? What does He want to do? And then

I go through testimonies, and the feeling of motivation and zeal now feels like it was in the beginning.

This is the same thing with marriages. Some people are the happiest on their wedding day. If only they look back at their wedding photos, it may help them to be more excited. That is why some people have renewed their vows. My wife and I go out on date nights every so often. Why? Otherwise, you'll get to the point where you just think, "Vanity upon vanity, all is vanity!" Those are the words of a disillusioned person and a frustrated person. You go back to the essence of your calling and ask yourself, "Why am I still serving God? Why am I giving to God? Why am I sacrificing my life to God?" If you do this, you'll always be motivated and inspiring to the people you lead.

The people we lead must never be more motivated than we are; otherwise, your leadership tenure is coming to an end. I'm not saying that you will suppress their own motivation; I am saying to double yours, and vision is one of the most potent tools for motivation. That's why God shows leaders more than the people they are leading so that they can stay inspired and motivated because there are more rivers to cross. When the people think it's time to rest, the leader already sees far ahead.

While I was working on certain projects, there were times that required me to scan every computer system in Edmonton for credit card information. I did this to ensure computer hackers did not find credit cards. At some point, I had about 5,000 credit cards and access to credit card information in my custody. And I thank God because He kept me. Sometimes I would sit there and just wonder what the reason for me doing this assignment was. Then, I would have to remind myself that I was rendering a service to all of Edmonton because I didn't want someone's information and identity stolen.

I was meditating on the essence of my work and how it positively affected people's lives. It was a lot of work and quite monotonous, but I stayed motivated once I reminded myself of the purpose behind my work. You'll always need someone else to motivate you if you don't understand why you're doing something. Leaders are commonly the chief motivators, or at least we are supposed to be!

When the AVL Team at CCCG was having difficulties with streaming, and people were having trouble connecting online to the service, amidst their frustration, I began inspiring the AVL Team and letting them know that they were playing a very important role. The encouragement helped them understand that they do make a difference. Those who lead the Worship Team are responsible for setting the atmosphere and ensuring that the presence of God is solid so that the Word can go forth and people can be blessed and refreshed. The job of the Continuous Improvement Team is to make the earth look like heaven and make things better so people can see God at work.

As leaders, we must know why we are doing what we are doing; otherwise, it will become a monotonous task, leading us to guilt-trip people doing the work and making them feel condemned. When you are given a new assignment, determine its role in the vision. The moment you connect the dots, that becomes your life, and you just keep revisiting it, and it will be difficult for you to lack motivation.

EMPATHY

Empathy is another way of showing high emotional intelligence. Empathy simply means having the ability to put yourself in somebody else's situation. This will help us develop people properly, challenge those who act unfairly, give constructive feedback, and listen to those who need it. Someone said that nobody cares how much you know until they know how much you care. That is empathy. And you can't really care if you don't put yourself into someone else's issues. I see how people do that every day; it's almost like they downplay others' situations: "I know your car broke down, but what's the big deal?" That is a sign of someone who lacks empathy. Empathy does not mean that you accept their response as right; you're just putting yourself in their situation.

There is a practical exercise that we can use. If I told you to draw the number three on your forehead, some of you would do it facing yourself, and some would do it facing me. If you do it facing me, you are drawing it for me to see, which is a sign of empathy. I didn't tell you to draw three in a specific direction, and I'm not saying that if you drew it for yourself, you lack empathy! It is just a sign that you are thinking of other people. That's love - thinking about other people.

Let's look at it from a more practical perspective. Let's say someone responsible for leading worship came late when they should have come early. That's unacceptable and not the way it should be. First of all, is the person sorry? Are they coming in with an attitude, or are they coming back sorrowful? Of course, you're not pleased or happy because that person should be reliable. Once you find someone to fill in the gap left by the late person, you can pay closer attention to determine the other person's situation.

Some leaders will focus on a person's absence and won't find someone else to take their place, so their work will also suffer. The work should be dealt with because it's the leader's responsibility. You should also look after the person that was involved with that. Putting yourself in people's situations, even if you are upset with someone because you had an expectation and they didn't meet it. You can choose not to shout at the person and just tell them you'll talk to them about it another day. It's very simple. This can only happen when there is self-regulation.

A wonderful person told me that my breathing was quite interesting and felt like it could be better. She sent me videos so that I could train by using my tummy and my diaphragm. One of the videos said that you release the air gradually and regulate the way the air is being released so that it comes outside nicely. In the same way, when we are angry, we know that we are not at the optimal level to address certain situations. It is okay to postpone when it is resolved, discussed, or dealt with. It's okay to do that.

I read that speaking words is like putting a nail on the wall. You can remove the nail by saying that you're sorry, but the hole is still there. As leaders, we have authority, and our words carry weight. Saying to someone that you're disappointed in them and that you don't think they could ever be trusted again because someone came late is too much. Even when they're trying to do better, your words will continue to ring in their mind and remind them that they cannot meet your expectations. That is already a barrier that can keep limiting them from taking steps forward. We need to ask God to help us and give us grace.

If people in the world can try to do these things, then we are in a way better place if we just apply certain principles. I am not saying that we don't have a right to be angry. I am saying that we are just thinking from their perspective.

One of the reasons why I can never judge anyone, no matter the sin that they commit, is because I know where I came from. It's like some clean Christians today have forgotten that, at some point, they were dirty. Some people who are free now have forgotten that they were bound. Is it because you are a leader that you now have the right to turn around and question people in a condescending manner? Absolutely not! Are we condoning what the people are doing? Never. I learned that God has the same expectations for all of us, but not at the same time.

A 10-year-old and a 2-year-old can be involved in breaking a plate, but the parent will scold the 10-year-old and allow the 2-year-old to go scot-free. Does that mean breaking the plate is right? No, but the younger one has not reached the age where they could be held accountable. Moses was told to speak to the rock, but he hit the rock and was not allowed to see the promised land. The Israelis messed up time and time again, and God kept on forgiving them because Moses had more experience with God than the Israelis ever had, so God had a higher expectation of him.

How else can we have empathy? Pay attention to people's body language, not just their words. As leaders, when we assign responsibilities and delegate tasks, we must be able to think about other people. For example, how I handle a leader with four children and certain responsibilities to fulfil before getting to church at 8:00 a.m. is different from how I handle a leader who is unmarried and has no children. It's about being able to understand where people are coming from.

There are times when it's very difficult to have empathy if you don't know their story. This is why it is important to know the people you are leading, to know their stories and have conversations with them, and to gain their trust so they can share things with you. Suppose you are driving, and someone cuts you off on the road, and you find out that they were rushing to the hospital because someone in the car just had a heart attack. Their action would suddenly seem easily forgivable. Knowing the people we're leading will help us to understand them better.

Let's say that you have someone who habitually comes late. Empathy at first says that it is okay. After a while, you will begin to take other steps because of empathy and love. If you put yourself in their shoes, you will wonder how this behaviour could affect them at work. Their reputation could be tainted. Because of empathy, I would take corrective and punitive action, even suspending individuals if necessary. What empathy prompts us to do may vary, but it should always be a factor. Empathy does not mean leading solely from the heart, which would allow emotions to dictate actions. God is love, but also just. Leading only with love may neglect the need for wisdom and balance in leadership.

SOCIAL SKILLS

On the topic of social skills, we'll touch on three things:

1. **Learn Conflict Resolution**
2. **Improve Your Communication Skills**
3. **Learn to Praise People**

Learn Conflict Resolution

Conflict resolution is an art. I learned something from a former FBI negotiator - it is the art of repeating to people what they said to make sure and confirm that you heard them. That is very effective in conflict resolution. A problem shared is a problem half-solved, so this person is already calming down because they feel heard. By the time you deal with how they're feeling, they would have already let it go, and then you can deal with the situation later. Conflict resolution can be as easy as just understanding where people are coming from. Don't inject your own ideas or expectations into it. Understand why they are frustrated.

Improve Your Communication Skills

What do I mean by this? I have realized that sometimes teachers and apostles believe that people should fill in the blanks and know what they are thinking because they are strategic people. They might think they had already had the conversation with the person, but they only had it with themselves.

Before I understood this about teachers and apostles, I was frustrated with people, being an apostle myself. The Holy Spirit knew my mind, but human beings didn't. I realized there were so many blanks, and I was expecting they would fill them in. I realized that this expectation wasn't fair, so I had to learn how to communicate with people. We need to remember that people are not in our minds. How will we know that they don't get it? When they say that they don't understand. The essence of communication is to make sure that the other person understands. If they don't understand, it means that the communication is not being done properly. When we are communicating, we should not only look at what people are saying, but we should also look for their full response to what we're saying.

If we are communicating with people who are not as confident, they could just start nodding. Although some people say they understand, I know they don't. So then I ask a question, but they can't give an answer. If it is leader to leader or colleague to colleague, it can seem condescending to ask them to summarize what you just talked about, but if you are speaking to someone you're mentoring and you're not confident that they understood what you said, then you can ask them to summarize what they heard. If it's accurate, you can move on, but if they missed something, you can fill in the blanks.

For most people, you can tell that they do not understand by their facial expressions. You can tell that they're trying to piece the information together. In that case, you would just help them. When you are clarifying, try not to be frustrated. Expressing that frustration can make it more difficult for people to understand because they are now anxious, knowing that they didn't get it, and they see that you're getting frustrated. In such a scenario, it adds more pressure to the meeting to understand it once you explain it again.

One of the things a person can do in taking personal responsibility is to decide to record the conversation they're having with someone. They could also write down notes so that they can go back, read it again, and then understand. There's nothing wrong with that. When some people meet with me, with my permission, they record the meeting so they can go back and listen to it and capture key details they may have missed during the conversation. If you don't have an answer to a question, you must be willing to say that you don't, but you will find the answer and get back to them.

Learn to Praise People

Regarding social skills, praising people can be delicate, as some may feel it is insincere. As a leader, giving earned praise can inspire team loyalty, but it must be done in a way that is well-received. Some may prefer private recognition, while others prefer public acknowledgment. We are all different, and understanding how individuals prefer to be praised is key. Additionally, giving praise may not always be appropriate if the recipient is not receptive. For instance, if someone appears downcast, addressing a different matter before giving praise may be more effective.

11

Impartation

It's good to be challenged if you want to be challenged, but not everybody can keep up with a fast pace. One of the reasons people find it challenging is that they want to hold onto pleasure while still doing everything else. They want to read, watch movies, and binge-watch Netflix. They want to have three-hour phone conversations about nothing while also being productive.

We host basic leadership classes at our church, and in the second class of the basic leadership course, we talked about prioritization. We discussed the principles of putting in the big rocks first, then filling the gaps with sand, and then filling up the rest with water. The big rocks represent the important things, and we should prioritize them. Where do you want to go in life? God has said that CCCG will be a reference point for many other ministries. He said that people would come here from all over the world to catch the fire of the Holy Spirit. This cannot just happen by doing things like everyone else does.

I was sharing with our ministry leaders one night that I went to bed one Sunday morning at 5:30 am, still had to be at church by 8 am, prepare for service at 9:30 am, work on my Ph.D. courses, rest a bit, attend leader's prayers, and have meetings. To take the lead in any aspect, we need to know where we are going, which will define the amount of work we need to put in. Not everyone wants to be a leader, so if I'm taking these drastic steps and someone sees it as too much work, their comments might seem loving, but you should ask them what they are trying to get to.

A lot was said about Kobe Bryant when he died. Many things were circulating on the internet about his commitment, drive, discipline, and consistency. Nobody ever gets to the top by accident. I read an article about the Stripe billionaires. Two of them were brothers in their early thirties, one was 17 years old, and the other was 19. They built a chip company and later sold it for millions of dollars. What was their background story? They were living in a farm area in Ireland and kept reading books since they didn't have many friends. Elon Musk had the same situation. He read so many books that there were no new books left in the library except encyclopedias, so he started reading those.

I can tell people who will excel in five years, and you don't need to be a prophet. You just need to look at their routine and see what they do every single day. It's easy for someone to hear something like this, get excited, and change their ways, but a week later, they're back to their old habits. We can't get anywhere worth going by doing what everyone else does. It's not possible.

I remember when I arrived in Canada and landed in Toronto. My uncle advised me against seeking factory work and getting caught up with that. He urged me to take my time and think about what I wanted to do in Canada. He said, "If you want to be a drug dealer or a criminal, you have everything at your disposal. But if you want to do extremely well, you also have everything at your disposal. I cannot choose for you. You must make your own choice." Every day, I strive to make good choices and encourage you to do the same.

We have covered ten different topics and discussed many things. Some people will carry on with business as usual, while others will be able to look back and say no to the things they used to allow in their lives. They will be able to cut off that person, stop watching that show, and get rid of those clothes. It's not that these things are bad, but I can't fill my head with them anymore. My purpose in life is to hear those words, "Well done, good and faithful servant." Every day, I take steps to ensure that I hear those words. There are some days when I miss the mark, but I keep asking God for His grace. So I beg you to make these ten lessons count by the special grace of God.

Right now, I can't imagine talking to someone on the phone for an hour anymore. When we begin to uncover these things, it may seem like we are under pressure, but that is good. There is good pressure and bad pressure. Bad pressure is called stress. Good pressure helps produce value. Some of us might agree that we perform better under pressure or with deadlines. When you have only one hour to finish a paper as opposed to a whole day, you will keep thinking you have time. I've learned to live life under pressure, which is why I enjoy doing many things simultaneously, such as being in school, writing books, and engaging in various other activities. It also protects me from sin because when David did not go to fight with the others, he saw Bathsheba and his life went downhill from there.

Being under pressure is very beneficial. I recall when I worked at Deloitte. Whenever we saw each other in the hallway, we would ask how we were doing, and we would always respond by saying we were keeping busy. Keep your head down, stay focused, and do what needs to be done. If you have a like-minded person that you can hold yourself accountable to, that would be helpful.

HOW TO IMPLEMENT YOUR LEARNINGS

When you are on the path of pursuing your vision and trying to implement all that you have learned in your life, the real question is how to sustain it.

VISION

Habakkuk 2:1-4, says to write down the vision so that you may run with it. Like I said earlier, I am not talking about a vision board that you develop and spend a lot of time on but never look at again. These vision boards are good, but make sure that your vision goes from being on paper to going in your heart. When you get a vision, you should be willing to die for it, as it becomes a part of your destiny, life, and identity merged with the vision that God has given you. When you get to this point, you don't need motivational videos for inspiration. I believe in inspiration, but not the way many people do. Many people listen to motivational speakers without focus, and it's almost like a drug for them.

GOALS

You need to set goals based on your vision. These goals are the programming for your vision. Then you need to put these goals into your calendar, reminders, or whatever app you use so that it translates into your daily schedule. However, some people put their alarms and reminders aside when they go off because they have not given themselves a reason to do what the reminder is saying they should do. The reason is the "why" behind the action. What is in it for you? Why should you get up at a particular time to pray? You need to know what you gain from doing these things. For example, why do you push yourself to pray? Because you would prefer to be proactive in dealing with the devil rather than being called after the fact. You would rather be proactive in knowing what is going to happen today so that you can deal with those things now as opposed to running behind schedule. It is a rallying cry to pay the price to do what you need to do.

It's very easy to get a desire, as God gave us an innate ability to cultivate the desire for anything. All it takes to begin to like a man you did not like before is if he is in your face every single day. Every one of us can succeed, but the issue is distractions, such as distractions from people, our past, and even our emotions. My life, to the glory of God, has been streamlined to the point that it's very simple. Anything that tries to shift me away from my calling cannot stay. It has to go, whether it's anything or anybody.

My calling is the reason why I am alive, and I will give an account to God. When my parents visited, it did not stop me from staying at church all day on Sundays and serving on Thursdays. It did not stop anything. When we had to be at church early, they also had to wake up early to be here on time. If they couldn't make it that early, I would have had to arrange for someone else to bring them to church. It's really just about having the determination you must succeed. You don't need anyone else's permission to succeed.

We are so privileged, as we have access to everything that is needed in order for us to be successful. I pray that you will be inspired and stay inspired in the precious name of Jesus. Five years from now, you will be higher than where you are now, and you will continue to go higher and higher in Jesus' name. Amen.

Epilogue

As we end this transformative journey through the pages of "Excellence in Leadership," we are reminded that pursuing excellent leadership is not a destination but a lifelong endeavour. It is a journey of growth, learning, and continuous refinement of our leadership skills and character. Throughout this book, we have explored crucial lessons that form the foundation of exceptional leadership.

The author, Emmanuel Adewusi, with his deep understanding and experience in leadership development, has guided us through the complexities and challenges leaders face in various spheres of influence. Drawing from his years of teaching basic and advanced leadership classes, Emmanuel has shared his wisdom and insights, rooted in his unwavering faith in Christ.

LESSON 1: We learned about the spiritual warfare that leaders face, recognizing the need to stand firm in our identity as children of God and rely on His strength to overcome every obstacle.

LESSON 2: Emmanuel reminded us of the spiritual authority we possess and the responsibility that comes with it, urging us to intentionally submit our will to God's word, the Holy Spirit, and authorized human authorities with integrity and humility.

LESSON 3: Emmanuel then took us on a journey of self-discovery and growth, emphasizing the vital importance of humility as the cornerstone of excellence in leadership.

LESSON 4: We explored servant leadership, embracing the transformative power of selflessness and empathy.

LESSON 5: We learned how to navigate the pressures that come from those we lead, finding wisdom and discernment in managing expectations while fostering a culture of trust and collaboration.

LESSON 6: Emmanuel provided valuable insights on avoiding burnout, prioritizing self-care, practicing spiritual disciplines, and seeking balance in our personal and professional lives.

LESSON 7: We were encouraged to run with the vision, persevering through challenges and staying focused on the ultimate goal.

LESSONS 8 & 9: Emmanuel unfolded a comprehensive exploration of leading with love, revealing the profound impact of love on our leadership. These lessons shed light on cultivating trust, growth, and empowering environments.

LESSON 10: We discovered the significance of emotional intelligence in leadership, understanding the power of self-awareness and empathy in fostering healthy relationships and effective communication.

LESSON 11: The Holy Spirit imparted leadership upon us. Learning the principles is one thing, but being able to apply them in every applicable context is another.

As we reflect on the journey we have embarked upon, we realize that the lessons learned here are not merely intellectual exercises but to be lived out in our daily lives as leaders. Emmanuel Adewusi, with his passion for equipping leaders, has provided us with valuable insights and sparked a desire for ongoing growth and transformation within us.

Remember, leadership is not just a title; it is a calling, a responsibility, and a privilege. May your leadership journey be marked by excellence, guided by the principles shared in these pages, and inspired by the transformative power of leading with love.

With gratitude for the wisdom shared in "Excellence in Leadership," let us rise to the challenges ahead, equipped with the lessons learned and empowered by the God who called us to lead. May our lives reflect the excellence and grace that comes from Him as we continue to inspire and empower those around us.

The journey continues. The impact deepens. And together, we transform the world through excellence in leadership.

Contact the Author

I know without a doubt that this book has been a blessing to you. I am looking forward to hearing your testimony.

You can contact me through email at emmanuel.adewusi@cc-cghq.org or visit emmanueladewusi.org for more information.

A Sinner's Prayer

Dear Heavenly Father,

I come to You in the Name of Jesus Christ.

You said in Your Word, "*Whosoever shall call upon the name of the Lord shall be saved.*" (Romans 10:13) I am calling on Your Name, so I know You have saved me now.

You also said that "*if you confess with your mouth the Lord Jesus and believe in your heart that God has raised Him from the dead, you will be saved. For with the heart one believes unto righteousness, and with the mouth, confession is made unto salvation.*" (Romans 10:9-10) I believe in my heart Jesus Christ is the Son of God. I believe that He was raised from the dead for my justification, and I confess Him now as my Lord and Savior.

Thank you, Lord, because now, I am saved!

Thank You, Lord, because I know you have heard my prayer. Thank You, Lord, because I am now born again.

Signed _____

Date _____

About the Author

Emmanuel Adewusi is the Founding and Lead Pastor of Cornerstone Christian Church Of God.

Called into ministry with the mandate to "bring restoration and transformation to all by teaching, preaching, and demonstrating the gospel of Jesus Christ," he is passionate to see lives restored and transformed the way God intended from the beginning of creation. He has a passion for the full counsel of the word of God, fellowship with the Holy Spirit, and being under spiritual authority.

He hosts several "Come and See" Conferences, with the goal to reach lost souls for Jesus Christ.

He authored the books "Now That You Are Born Again, What Next?", "The Blessings of Being Under Spiritual Authority", "A Disciplined Life", "Interconnected Systems: A Wisdom Manual", "Channels of Grace: How to Seamlessly Connect & Stay Connected with God", "It Can Be Done", and other impactful titles. He has also released albums titled "Divine Encounter", "Realms", "Declare", and many more on the way.

Emmanuel Adewusi is joyfully married to his wife, Ibukun Adewusi, and together, they are building a thriving Christ-centered family.